Little

BIRDIE

Little
BIRDIE

Bethany Thompson

YorkshirePublishing
www.yorkshirepublishing.com
Write Now.

ISBN: 978-1-947247-25-3
Little Birdie
Copyright © 2013 by Bethany Thompson

Yorkshire Publishing
3207 South Norwood Avenue
Tulsa, Oklahoma 74135
www.YorkshirePublishing.com
918.394.2665

Dedicated to God, the most incredible author of all, who is writing my story.

Thanks to my sister Grace, my own personal editor, and the rest of my family for believing in me and encouraging me to dream big.

1. Haying Season

"Esther! Not so fast around the corner."

Fifteen-year-old Esther Sullivan tightened the reins. The team of horses slowed, and she guided them alongside the row of hay before pulling them to a stop.

Her brother David, three years older, walked beside the wagon, pitching forkfuls of hay up to their father, who pressed it into the corners. Esther waited until David was even with her before she urged the horses forward again.

After they'd taken another turn around the field, Esther's father called out, "This load is big enough. Let's take it to the barn."

David climbed into the wagon and flopped down on the hay, wiping his face on his shirtsleeve.

"Here, Esther, I'll drive."

Esther smiled up at her father. "Thanks, Dad."

She handed him the reins and tumbled back into the wagon to stretch out beside David. Brushing away the hay that was tickling her nose, she rested her chin on her hands. The bright June sun warmed her back, and the trill of a red-winged blackbird floated across the still air. She closed her eyes, letting her tired muscles relax.

The wagon stopped in front of the barn, and David swung to the ground, grabbing his pitchfork on the way.

Esther jumped down and walked to where a harnessed horse stood. "Ready, Triangle?" she asked the mare, watching the small window above her where the hay fork track began.

After a minute, David looked out. "Go ahead, Esther," he called down. "We're all set."

Climbing into the wagon, Esther closed the steel jaws of the fork around some hay and clucked to Triangle. The mare moved forward, propelling the load up into the barn.

"That's far enough!" came a muffled shout.

Esther had jumped to the ground, and now she grabbed Triangle's reins, stopping the horse. She pulled the rope that was connected to the jaws of the fork, releasing the hay into the mow.

Triangle trotted around the wagon, bringing the fork back down, and stopped where she had started, ready to begin all over again. The process was monotonous, but Esther was glad she didn't have to be up in the hot, dusty mow.

Two wagonloads later, Esther closed the steel jaws of the fork around the last of the hay in the wagon and shook the reins to get Triangle moving. Her mouth was dry, and her arms were itchy, but she sighed with relief. *We won't have to do this again for a while!*

David came out of the barn, wiping his face and neck with a grimy handkerchief. "I am so hot," he burst out. "Let's go swimming in the creek."

"Yes, let's." Esther turned to her father. "Will you go with us?"

He started unhitching Triangle. "Are you sure you want me to go with you?"

"Of course we do," David spoke up. "Come on, Dad. I'll only dunk you once, I promise."

"Only once?" He looked over at Esther, his eyes twinkling. "I can't pass that up."

Esther helped her father and David put the horses away, and then they all hurried across the hay field to the creek in their woods. David pulled his boots off and jumped in, hollering that the water was cold.

Esther stuffed her stockings inside her shoes and left them beside her father's and David's boots.

As she waded in, David called out, "Hurry up, Esther. You are always the last one in."

"I am not," she protested, splashing him. Then she slipped and lost her balance, plopping into the water with a little shriek. "It's freezing!" She shivered as the cool water soaked into her clothes.

David grinned and splashed her back. Esther shook the water from her ears and swam downstream to shallower water. When she turned around, she saw her father, wet and spluttering, charge David. David lunged downstream, yelling.

"Esther!" her father called. "I'm holding his legs. You push his head under."

David thrashed his legs and arms. "No!"

Esther laughed. "It'll help you cool off, like you wanted." She pushed him under.

David came up coughing and spluttering.

"All right, let's head back now." Esther's father glanced at her as he waded toward the bank, squeezing water from his shirt. "Mama might need your help."

Esther wrung as much water as she could from her long skirt before following her father and David out of the woods. As they approached their two-story, white house, Esther saw smoke curling from the stone chimney.

Mama must have already started supper, she thought. Snatches of song drifted out an open window, and Esther recognized one of the hymns they had sung in church the day before.

She hurried up the porch steps and slipped through the dining room into the kitchen. "We're done, Mama!" she burst out.

The singing stopped, and her mother turned from the wooden table where she was sorting a bucket of new potatoes. Her blue eyes sparkled.

"Finished with all that hay? That's wonderful! Did you have a good swim in the creek?" She smiled good-naturedly at their dripping clothes.

"We sure did." David ran his fingers through his black curls. "On a day like today, that creek is…ahh!" He sighed with pleasure.

Esther grinned at him and then turned to her mother. "I'm going to go find some dry clothes, Mama, but I'll be back to help with supper."

She went upstairs, changed into a calico dress, and gathered up her wet clothing. Sticking her head in at David's open door, Esther saw him sitting on his bed, lacing up his boots.

"Would you like me to take care of your laundry?" she asked, motioning to the clothes strewn about the floor.

David gave her a delighted grin and nodded. "Thank you, Esther."

She added his dripping clothes to her pile and started down the stairs, holding the laundry away from her. Just as the fourth step creaked under her feet, the door beside the foot of the stairs opened, and her father came out.

"Here, Dad, I can hang out your clothes." She took his wet laundry and grinned at him. "Your hair is sticking up."

"Oh, yes. I forgot to comb it." Her father turned back into his room.

Esther hurried outside. She wrung out the clothes and flung them over the clothesline. Noticing a patch of daisies beside the springhouse creek, she went over and picked some.

When she returned to the kitchen, her mother turned from washing potatoes. "Oh, Esther. My favorite!"

Esther held out the daisies. "I'll finish the potatoes."

"Thank you, sweetie." Her mother took the flowers with a smile and kissed her forehead.

When supper was ready and they were all seated at the table, Esther's father asked a blessing on the food and thanked the Lord for all the hay they'd put up.

"At church yesterday I heard that Joshua Pritchard finally left to join Lincoln's army," David said. He slid the serving bowls toward his plate and helped himself to a generous portion of fresh green beans and new potatoes.

"He's wanted to ever since the beginning of the war," David continued, "but he had agreed to help his uncle until the end of June, and his father wouldn't let him break his word. His uncle let him off a week early, though, and now he's on his way to enlist. I wish I could've gone with him. I want to get in on the excitement before it's over."

Esther stopped chewing and glanced at her parents. When the war broke out three months ago, her father had told them he wasn't going to enlist.

"David," his father said slowly, "after you have considered everything involved in war and what the Bible says about treating others the way you want to be treated, are you sure you still want to be a part of it?"

David shifted, staring down at his plate. "All I know is..." He paused. "It's embarrassing to be the only able-bodied man in Kirksville—and probably all of Southwestern Pennsylvania—who hasn't signed up. People are asking me why I haven't enlisted yet, and I have a hard time knowing what to tell them." He shook his head and went back to eating.

"David, are you going to take the team back to the Washburns tonight?" Esther asked, breaking the silence. "If you hurry you should get back about the same time we finish the chores."

"And then we can all have devotions together," her father finished.

2. Something's Wrong

Esther carried a stack of plates into the kitchen and set them down beside the washtub. As she was fetching the milk pail, her mother came in.

"The Washburns didn't put their garden out very early this year," she said. "We could give them some of our potatoes for letting us use their team and wagon."

"That is a wonderful idea, Mama." Esther set the tin pail on the table. "I'll fill a bag from the bin in the cellar, and David can take it with him."

The cellar was under a trap door in the kitchen. Esther filled one of the empty sacks beside the potato bin and lugged it back up the steps. She trudged outside with it, humming the song her mother had been singing earlier.

The barn was cool after the heat of the day, and Esther breathed in the aroma of the newly-cut hay in the mow. David and her father were in the two stalls beside Triangle's harnessing the Washburns' team.

Esther slipped in with Triangle, resting her arms on the top board of the dividing wall. "David, Mama is sending a sack of potatoes along with you for the Washburns."

David glanced over the back of his horse. "They sure deserve it."

"I put it in the back of the wagon," she said as he led the horses outside. "Don't stay for any of Peter's stories," she called after him.

Pushing through the back door of the barn into their fenced pasture, she called, "Milksop. Here, girl."

The dark brown cow was at the other end near the woods. Esther propped the door open and started running, groaning as her sore muscles protested. *I'm glad this haying season is finished.*

"Come now, Milksop, to the barn," she huffed, prodding the grazing cow.

After tying Milksop in the stanchion, she sat on the wooden stool and began milking.

When she was almost finished, her father came over. "I fed and watered Triangle and the chickens," he said.

Milksop shifted her feet, bumping the bucket.

"Milksop, hold still," Esther scolded.

Her father squatted down on the other side of the cow. "I remember when she was a calf and you named her Milksop because she drank so much milk."

Esther could tell he was smiling as he continued. "And I remember the look on your face when I explained that milksop means coward."

Esther stripped the last of the milk from the cow. "Oh, Daddy, that was a long time ago."

Her father stood up and grinned at her. "I'll put Milksop out for you."

In the springhouse Esther strained the milk into one of the stone crocks in the cooling trough. She found her mother sitting in her rocking chair in the living room doing some mending. Esther sat down on the sofa and picked up the pair of socks she was knitting for David.

Her father came in, took the leather-bound Bible from the fireplace mantel, and sat in a chair beside Mama. Before long David plunked down beside Esther, and their father read aloud a chapter from the Bible.

That night in her room Esther heard a knock on her door. "Come in," she called, turning back her quilts.

The door opened, and her mother came in, struggling with a large pitcher. Esther hurried to help her.

"Mama, you shouldn't carry heavy things up the stairs," she said. "Let me take care of filling our pitchers."

"I think I will from now on." Her mother sighed, leaning against the door. "I can't do as much as I used to, and before long I probably won't be good for anything other than talking."

Surprised by the discouragement in her mother's voice, Esther spilled some water into the washbasin as she filled her pitcher. "Don't say that, Mama." She frowned, setting the larger pitcher on the floor. Handing her mother her comb, she sat down on the bed. "Will you please comb my hair?"

Her mother took the comb and pulled it through Esther's black hair.

After a moment of silence, Esther turned to look up at her. "I love you, Mama."

Her mother's face brightened, and she hugged Esther. "I love you too, honey," she said. "And I didn't mean to sound so glum. I'm just tired."

"Well, I do a lot of the housework, but I still need you to tell me how," Esther said.

"Not really." Esther's mother sat down on the bed beside her. "You know more than you think."

Esther flopped back on the bed. "But, Mama, it wouldn't be any fun to take care of the house and garden without you."

Her mother smiled and pulled Esther back up, putting an arm around her. "Working with you is special. Even though you are nearly grown up, you still want to be my little girl. But you have the skills you need, and I'm proud of the young lady you've become."

Esther returned her mother's hug. "Thank you, Mama."

After a bit her mother stood up, handing the comb back to Esther. "I should go fill David's pitcher," she said, starting toward the door. "Thankfully mine is lighter now."

Esther grinned. "Goodnight, Mama."

"Goodnight, sweetheart." Her mother picked up the pitcher and went out.

"A photograph?" Esther repeated, staring at her father over her glass of milk the next morning. "Wonderful! But," she hesitated, "doesn't that cost a lot?"

Her father smiled. "I thought we could make it David's birthday present a week early, because the photographer is passing through right now." He smiled at David. "We'll leave for town as soon as we've done the chores."

David grinned. "Great! I'll finally get to see how they take photographs."

After helping her mother with the dishes, Esther went upstairs to put on her best dress. *I can hardly believe it,* she thought, hugging herself. *A real photograph of all of us!*

As she braided her hair, she glanced out the window and saw David riding Triangle bareback in the pasture. After he had gone around the fence several times, he pulled the mare up at the barn and slid off her back. Esther knew what was coming next and leaned forward, pushing back the blue and white curtain.

Triangle reared up on her hind legs, pawing the air with her forelegs for a moment before coming back down. David stepped closer and rubbed her neck, then led her into the barn.

Esther smiled and dropped the curtain, hurrying downstairs.

Her mother came out of her bedroom wearing a beautiful light blue dress with darker trimming. "You look lovely, sweetheart." She pulled on her white gloves. "Let's go see if your father and David are ready."

"I rather doubt they are." Esther straightened her mother's necklace. "I just saw David riding Triangle."

She followed her mother outside and saw her father and David hitching Triangle to the wagon. David glanced over.

"We're almost ready." He walked the reins back to the wagon and stopped beside them, holding his hand out to his mother. "May I offer my assistance to this beautiful lady?"

Esther smiled, watching her mother's eyes brighten as she took David's hand.

"You may," she said, lifting her skirt away from the wheel. "I am honored to be assisted by such a handsome, thoughtful gentleman."

When she was seated, David turned to Esther. "Can I help you up too?" His blue eyes twinkled.

Esther grasped his hand, raising her eyebrows at him. "Doesn't the handsome, thoughtful gentleman have any compliments for me? And are you going in those clothes?"

David laughed. "No. I'll be right back."

He ran to the house and returned several minutes later with his hair combed and wearing his Sunday coat. Handing his father a similar black coat, he swung himself into the back of the wagon. Esther scooted to the edge of the seat to make more room as her father climbed up. He slapped the reins over Triangle's back, and they drove out the lane.

In town Esther shifted, watching the photographer adjust the tripod under his camera. Her parents were sitting in two chairs, and she and David were positioned behind them.

This isn't as easy as I expected, she thought. *We will probably look grumpy in the photograph since we've had to hold still for so long.*

"I'm ready," the photographer announced at last, sticking his head under a dark cloth attached to his camera. "This shouldn't take much longer."

Esther gave a little sigh of relief and shot a quick glance at David.

He rolled his eyes, making a face at the black box in front of them.

Esther snickered, just as a flash erupted from the device the photographer was holding out toward them.

"I'm finished," he told them, emerging from under the cloth. "It will take me a day or so to develop the images."

Esther stared at him and then punched at her brother's arm. "David, you made me laugh."

He grinned. "What's wrong with that? Did you want to look as sober as the rest of us?"

When her father fetched the photographs from town two days later, Esther ran out to meet him.

"How did they turn out?" she asked, taking hold of Triangle's bridle.

Her father handed her a package. "See for yourself," he told her, swinging down from the saddle.

Esther ripped open the package and carefully took out two photographs. "David looks very grown up," she said, examining her brother's individual picture. "And I look ridiculous!" she exclaimed, seeing the comical expression on her face in the family photograph.

"What about the rest of us?" her father asked, stepping up beside her. "Or are you only concerned about yourself?"

Esther gave him a small smile, seeing the twinkle in his eyes. "I guess that did sound rather selfish. Other than the face I'm making, I suppose it is a nice photograph."

He grinned, turning to lead Triangle to the barn. "Take them to the house to show your mother. I'll send David in too. He'll be glad to take a break from hoeing."

"Do you think we could have a taffy pull this winter, Mama?"

Esther was helping her mother pick green beans, two and a half weeks later, and her mouth watered as she remembered the gooey candy they'd made at the Washburns' the previous winter.

"That is a wonderful idea! I'm sure we can." Her mother straightened up, wiping her forehead. "It is so warm today."

Esther glanced up. Her mother's face was flushed.

"I'll finish," Esther offered. "You can go inside and rest."

"Thank you, dear." Her mother smiled at her and left the garden.

Esther continued picking beans, frowning at the green and yellow leaves. For the past week her mother had often laid down in the middle of the day. Yesterday Esther had done all the washing and most of the ironing.

Picking up the buckets of beans when she finished, she headed for the house. Glancing toward where her father and David were hoeing in the cornfield, she caught sight of their heads above the rippling green.

Esther did not see her mother in the living room, so she went to her parents' bedroom. She saw her mother in bed, curled under a quilt. Her breathing sounded uneven, and she moaned.

Esther tiptoed closer. "Mama?" she whispered. "Are you asleep?"

Her mother shook her head and coughed.

Esther reached down to feel her forehead. "You have a fever. Shall I sponge your face and hands?"

"Get your father," her mother whispered. "And send David for the doctor." She coughed again.

Esther forgot to breathe for a moment. "I–I will, Mama," she promised.

She was panting when she reached her father in the cornfield. "Something's wrong with Mama," she gasped.

Her father dropped his hoe. "What happened?" he demanded, taking her elbow. "Is she hurt?"

"She's sick, Dad! She wants David to go for the doctor!" Esther clutched his arm. "What's wrong with her?" she whimpered.

"The doctor!" Her father glanced at David and started running for the house. "Hurry, son."

David sprinted toward the pasture. He leaped over the fence, caught Triangle, and rode her to the gate.

When Esther looked back at her father, he had already reached the house.

3. God's Answer

Esther sat on the porch, snapping beans for supper and watching the road. As soon as she saw Triangle cantering toward their house, she jumped to her feet and leaned over the railing. "David! How far behind you is the doctor?"

Then she saw that his shoulders were slumped.

"The doctor isn't coming, is he?" Her voice trailed off in disappointment.

David shook his head. "He wasn't home. His wife will send him as soon as possible, but we shouldn't expect him before morning."

Tomorrow morning! Esther let out a long breath and kicked at the railing.

Her father stepped out onto the porch, a question on his face. When she repeated David's news, the furrows in his forehead deepened, and he went back into the bedroom.

Esther took the beans to the kitchen, strung the rest of them together to dry, and finally settled on the sofa with her knitting. As she stared at the recent photographs propped up on the mantel, David came in and plopped down beside her.

He watched her knit for a moment and then said, "You should probably start making supper."

Esther didn't slow her needles. "I'm not hungry."

"I'm not either, but—" David's stomach growled. He stared down at it, and Esther laughed at the half-amused, half-annoyed expression on his face.

"All right," she said. "I'll go make supper."

When the food was ready, Esther dished out a plate for her father and carried it to the bedroom. "Does Mama want anything?" she whispered, looking past her father to her feverish mother.

He shook his head.

At the table David shuddered. "Oh, bother!" he exclaimed, helping himself to more meat pie. "This house is too quiet."

Esther nodded but didn't say anything. *I just wish we knew what is wrong with Mama,* she thought.

It was dark outside by the time she and David had finished the chores, so they went up to their rooms. But Esther couldn't sleep. She tiptoed downstairs and sat on the floor. Leaning against the wall by her parents' bedroom door, she wrapped her arms around her knees. Her heart sank as she listened to her mother's cough.

Light streamed through the window when Esther awoke. She yawned and stretched, wincing at her cramped muscles. *Mama…I wonder if Mama is any better.* She glanced around and saw her brother.

David was asleep on the bottom step, slumped against the wall. She stared at him, letting her numb legs slide to the floor.

He was still wearing his threadbare trousers and blue shirt from yesterday.

She stood unsteadily and tried to step past him. Her foot bumped his arm, and he woke up, mumbling something.

Esther sat down beside him, laying her head against his shoulder. "You came down too."

He nodded. "You were already asleep. Your snoring sounded like a bumblebee in a flower." He grinned.

Esther nudged him with her elbow. "I don't snore."

"You're never awake to hear yourself, so how would you know?" David shifted away from her. "But I made up the part about bumblebees. It sounded good, didn't it?"

Esther laughed and then covered her mouth. "We'd better go upstairs before we wake Mama and Dad."

David nodded and helped her up. "If they're sleeping," he whispered. "Unless Mama was feeling better, Dad probably sat up with her."

Esther sighed, and he added, "Don't worry, Little Birdie. The doctor is going to come this morning."

The familiar nickname made her feel better. "You're right," she said as they went up the stairs. "I should stop worrying."

She changed into a clean dress and twisted her thick braid into a bun. But when she poured water from her pitcher into the washbasin and washed her face, she didn't feel quite as refreshed as usual. As she went to make breakfast, she saw her father on the sofa reading the Bible.

"How is Mama?" she asked, stopping in the living room doorway.

Her father looked up, his eyes tired. "I sat up with her most of the night, and I think she's about the same."

Esther bit her lip and went into the kitchen.

The doctor came while they were eating breakfast. Esther's father met him at the door, and they went into the bedroom together.

Esther pushed the food around on her plate and glanced at David. All she could hear through the bedroom door were muffled voices. At last the men reappeared.

"I'm sorry, Richard," the doctor said quietly, his dark eyes sympathetic. "I wish there was more I could do."

"Thank you, Doctor Cunningham. I appreciate you coming out here."

Esther's father showed the doctor out and stood for a moment, leaning against the closed door. Esther stood up, and he turned toward them.

"David and Esther, you know that Mama has never regained her strength from her fall last summer when she hurt her back and was sick for so long."

He paused, searching their faces. They nodded, and he continued. "Now she has a severe case of influenza, and her body is too weak to fight it. Doctor Cunningham gave her some medicine, but he says she only has a few more days to live." His voice trembled.

Esther stared at her father, hearing Doctor Cunningham's carriage rattle out the lane. She swallowed hard. *Mama isn't going to get better?*

She glanced down at her unfinished breakfast and over at her brother's plate of uneaten food.

Their father had gone back into the bedroom. David helped Esther put the food away and wash the dishes before going out to hoe the corn. Esther took the sewing basket and her knitting and knocked on her parents' door.

When her father opened the door, she whispered, "May I sit with Mama so you can rest?"

The lines across his forehead relaxed. "Thank you, Esther. But wake me if she gets worse." He went out and closed the door.

Esther sat down on the chair beside the bed, and her mother gave her a small smile. Esther squeezed her ball of yarn and blinked back tears.

"Oh, Mama, it doesn't make any sense. How could you have gotten influenza when none of the rest of us did?"

Her mother sighed. "Remember that visiting family in church last month? Doctor Cunningham said that one of their girls had just recovered from influenza. So you were exposed to it too, but you didn't get sick because you are strong and healthy."

"But how can you be sick enough to die?" Esther touched her mother's hand. "I want you here."

"I want to be here with you too, honey." Her mother's lip quivered, and tears stood in her eyes. "But God reminded me that our lives here are just for a moment, and then we will be in heaven with him and each other forever."

Esther nodded and swallowed hard. "David and I prayed that God would make you better."

Her mother's eyes softened. "Thank you, sweetheart. God might not answer the way you want him to, though. I used to think I could control him with my prayers, but I realized that if I could control him, he wouldn't be God."

She glanced at the basket of mending on the floor beside Esther. "Can I help with any of that mending?"

Esther swiped her hand across her wet cheeks. "Are you sure you want to?" she asked. "Shouldn't you just rest?"

Her mother sighed. "I've *been* resting. Isn't there one of your father's shirts that needs a button sewn back on? That should be easy enough for me to do."

"All right." Esther leaned over to dig through the basket.

She sat beside her mother for the rest of the morning, knitting and mending some of the other clothes in the sewing basket. "Should I wake Dad to come sit with you?" she asked when she needed to go get lunch ready.

Her mother shook her head. "No. I will be fine by myself."

The next several days were much the same. Her mother's fever was higher and she coughed more during the night. She couldn't seem to keep anything down, not even the broth Esther made for her. Esther sat with her mother every morning so her father could sleep, and in the afternoons she picked and washed more green beans, stringing them up to dry.

David spent most of his time in the cornfield and did all the chores. Esther was glad they ate and had devotions together in her parents' bedroom. But she felt helpless watching her mother grow weaker.

One afternoon Esther was in the kitchen chopping carrots and onions for supper. She filled a cup with water for her mother and went to the bedroom.

As Esther entered her mother was coughing and motioned to the cup. Esther helped her sit up to drink and noticed that her mother was running a high fever. She fetched some cool water and a cloth and sponged her mother's face and hands for nearly an hour. But it didn't seem to help.

"Mama, I am going to get Dad," she said at last, wondering if she sounded as scared as she felt.

Her mother's thin body shook with another coughing fit. Esther hurried to the living room where her father was asleep on the sofa.

"Dad, please come," she said urgently, touching his shoulder.

He was awake in an instant and rushed to the bedroom.

She followed him and heard her mother say, "I think I'm... going."

Esther's heart stopped for a moment before beating faster.

"Esther, go get David," her father commanded. "And hurry!"

Esther flew out onto the porch. "David!" she hollered, her panic spilling into her voice. "Come quickly!"

After staring toward her for a moment, David came running from the cornfield, clearing all three porch steps in one leap. They entered the bedroom together.

Esther paused inside the doorway, seeing her parents with their arms around each other.

Her mother beckoned them closer. "I love you all so much," she whispered. "You must go on with your lives, even though I won't be here with you." Her voice trembled, but her blue eyes were steady.

"David." She touched his dark curls when he knelt beside the bed. "Be a man after God's own heart, like your namesake."

She took Esther's cold hand into hers, hot and dry with fever. "Become the woman God wants you to be, Esther, and never lose your sensitivity for others.

"And you must all join me in heaven. God wants you there even more than I do."

Esther squeezed the hand in hers as her mother sank back. Her eyes drifted closed, and her face lit up. "I can see him! He's coming to take me home."

She whispered, "Jesus," and smiled so sweetly that Esther felt a strange calm inside where she'd been scared.

Her mother's smile faded, leaving a peaceful expression. As Esther stared at her mother's closed eyes, she felt the hot hands in hers grow cold. Into her dazed mind crept the realization that she would never feel her mother's arms around her again, never hear her laugh or see her smile.

Her heart twisted, and the ache in her throat made her eyes water. A tear trickled down her cheek, and she collapsed against the bed, sobbing, "Mama, no. Don't leave. Mama, please."

"Oh, Esther," her father said softly, touching her arm. "David, will you take her to her room? She looks exhausted."

David pulled Esther to her feet and helped her up the stairs. She leaned against him, still crying. When they reached her room, he took off her shoes and stockings and tucked her into bed as if she were a child. She was worn-out from the strain of the past week, but her pillow was damp with tears before she fell asleep.

It was dark when she awoke, feeling sore and miserable. As she laid there the clock on the mantel downstairs donged ten times. Everything came rushing back to her.

Her mother was dead. Gone forever.

She cried herself to sleep again.

4. Time to Let Go

In the morning Esther found out what David had done after tucking her into bed. He had gone into town with Triangle and the wagon, bought planks for a coffin, and asked the minister to come late that afternoon for the funeral. He also told their closest friends and neighbors and asked them to spread the word.

But that wasn't the only news he brought. When Esther came down to make breakfast, wishing she could stay in bed, all David could talk about was the battle near Bull Run in Virginia the day before.

Esther and her father picked at their food as David described in detail how the North had been soundly defeated. He had already done the chores, so when they finished eating, her father took him out to show him where to dig the grave.

Esther shuddered, thinking of her mother lying cold and silent in the bedroom, so different from her usual warm, cheerful self. Tears ran down Esther's cheeks as she heated water and washed the dishes. She had been washing only three plates for the past six days, but this time it was more depressing.

Her father came back in as she was wiping the table. "David and I made a coffin last night. Will you help me get Mama ready for—" He choked on the last words and didn't finish.

Esther's throat ached, and she dropped the dishrag to squeeze his hand. "Of course, Daddy."

She and her father spent the next hour preparing her mother's body and putting her in the coffin. Esther kept swallowing her sobs until her father went outside. Then she shut the bedroom door and slumped against it, crying until no more tears came.

Going to the coffin, she gazed at her mother's calm face. When the clock donged the hour, Esther finally stirred and hugged her, crushing the forget-me-not in her mother's hands.

As people arrived that afternoon for the funeral, Esther stood beside her father to greet them. Her closest neighbor, Mrs. Washburn, brought a loaf of fresh bread and some soup.

"It's for your supper, Esther," she said. "I'm sure you won't feel like working in a lonely kitchen tonight, so all you have to do is warm the soup and slice the bread. Be sure to let us know if there is anything else we can do for you," she added, giving Esther a gentle hug.

Esther clung to her for a moment, touched by her thoughtfulness.

When the minister arrived, Esther's father, David, Mr. Washburn, and a few other men carried the coffin out to the gravesite. Esther glanced around. Her father had chosen a spot beyond the pasture and fields near the woods.

The minister read several passages from his Bible and said what a blessing her mother had been to the community and how much the townsfolk would miss her. Esther didn't hear most of it.

The men lowered the coffin into the ground, and Esther took a deep breath as a tear slid down her cheek.

Two days passed slowly. Esther poured water into the basin on the kitchen table and scrubbed the dirt from her hands. She had been in the garden all afternoon, hilling potatoes and weeding carrots. After pitching the water out the window, she opened the trap door to the cellar and started down the stairs to fetch some vegetables for soup. She nearly tripped on something and stopped, peering closer in the dim light. There sat the bowls of carrots and onions she had chopped the day her mother died.

Esther picked up the bowls and shook them. The vegetables were dry and withered. *Just the way I feel,* she thought as she carried them out to the chickens.

David and her father continued to hoe the corn, but David's restlessness worried Esther. The men who came to the funeral had told him more about the Battle of Bull Run and the Northern army's need for young men.

David wouldn't enlist without Dad's permission, she reassured herself. *Not David. And Dad would never say he could go.*

But nine days after her mother's funeral, she was weeding onions when David came running toward her, his face shining.

"Esther! I'm finally going!" He turned a somersault and laughed, pulling her up from the dirt. "Dad said I could!"

"Going where?" Esther stared at him, a thread of fear snaking through her.

"To join Lincoln's army! I can't wait! I'm leaving early tomorrow morning. Say, could you pack some food for me?"

Esther nodded, blinking speechlessly up at him. She took a step closer and threw her arms around his middle, pressing her head against his chest. *Why do you have to leave, David?*

He hugged her back and then ran to the house—to pack, he said. Esther cried that night, but the next morning her brother was still so excited about going that she smiled for him as she gave him a good-bye hug.

She watched him stride away with his clothes and the food she had given him wrapped in the blanket slung over his shoulder. When he reached the big oak near the road, she called his name and ran after him.

"David," she panted, running up and grabbing his hand. "I forgot to tell you that I'll miss you. Write to me!"

He smiled into her worried eyes. "Of course, Little Birdie. I wouldn't forget." Then he squeezed her fingers and looked serious. "I'll be fine, I promise. I'll miss you too, you know that. Take care of Dad and Triangle, all right?"

"I will." She let go of his hand. "Good-bye."

When he disappeared around a bend, she went back to the house and found her father sitting on the porch steps.

"Why did you let him go?" she asked quietly, sitting below him and gazing toward Mama's distant grave.

Her father took a deep breath and let it out slowly. "I cannot force him to believe the way I do, and I cannot force him to stay here. So I said I wouldn't stand in his way." He sighed again. "It's better this way. He will want to come back home, whereas if he had run off, it would be harder for him to face me."

Esther nodded and leaned against his leg.

"I only hope that he will get his fill of it soon." Esther's father reached down and smoothed her hair away from her forehead. "And come back to us."

With David gone, Esther's father did all the chores and spent most of every day hoeing the corn.

One day as he was helping her hill the last of the potatoes, she leaned on her hoe. "Dad, have you changed your mind about David? Are you sorry you let him go?"

Her father shook his head. "No," he said. "I know I made the right decision."

Esther nodded and continued hoeing. *Then he must be missing Mama. He's been so quiet—almost moody.*

That night as she lay in bed, she heard him pacing below in his room. Wrapping a quilt around her shoulders, she eased out of bed and tiptoed to the landing, noticing that he had stopped. Last night he had paced for over an hour, and she hadn't been able to sleep.

The door creaked open, and she heard his footsteps on the porch. The clock donged eleven times as she descended the stairs to look out the window. Esther's forehead wrinkled. Her father was halfway across the field.

She slipped out to the porch and sat down in a corner, watching him through the railing.

He climbed the big rock not far from her mother's grave and stretched his fists to the sky. "Why, God? Why?" he yelled.

Moonlight silhouetted his figure, and in the stillness Esther's heart echoed his question. She burst into tears, the unfairness of losing her mother filling her with an ache stronger than ever.

Gradually her sobs lessened, and she fell into an uneasy sleep, her dreams haunted by her mother's face. When she awoke and remembered where she was, she stared out to where she had last seen her father.

He was no longer on top of the rock but kneeling beside it. She sighed and stood up to go inside. As she climbed the stairs, the clock on the mantel donged twice.

Dad has been out there for three hours, she realized as she crawled into bed.

Esther watched her father come in from chores the next morning as she set a bowl of fresh blueberries on the table. "What happened?" she asked.

He glanced at her as he sat down. "What do you mean?"

She shrugged. "You're not upset with God anymore."

His mouth turned up in a crooked smile. "Last night," he said slowly, "I was remembering so many things about your mother.

Dancing with her that first time in South Carolina, the way her hair looked in the wind, her singing, the taste of her strawberry preserves, how upset she would get when I put snow on her neck…"

He looked up half-guiltily at Esther and chuckled. Esther gazed at him, her mind flooding with memories of her own. She sat down and put her chin in her hand.

He stared out the window. "What if I had never met her? All those colorful memories would just be gray places in my life. She was the best—" His jaw tightened, and Esther felt a lump in her throat.

"She was the best woman God could have brought into my life," her father finished after a moment. "And if he hadn't, I wouldn't have you now, or David." He looked into Esther's eyes. "It hurts terribly to realize she won't ever be here again, but it would've been much worse to not have her at all. I'm grateful, Esther, forever grateful that God gave us the time together that he did. And today at least, my thankfulness is stronger than anything else."

Esther nodded, a tear spilling down her cheek. "It's just so hard to think of her without feeling hurt inside."

Her father reached out and took her hand. "God did not promise that everything in life would be easy, sweetheart, only that he would be with us when it's hard. And he is. He's here with us."

Esther nodded again, trying to believe it.

Later when they were washing the dishes, he said, "We should sort Mama's clothes this morning. What you won't be able to use we should give away. That is what she would have wanted."

Esther glanced up at him. "Are you sure you're ready to do that? I mean…I guess *you* are ready, but—" She broke off and looked down.

Her father cupped her chin in his hand and gently turned her face until she met his eyes. "Would you rather do it some other time? I don't mind waiting."

Esther sighed and shook her head. "We might as well do it today," she said, swallowing hard. "Waiting won't make it any easier."

She followed him into his bedroom, and they began sorting her mother's dresses, packing the nicest ones into a trunk.

"Maybe I should wear some of these." Esther held up one of her mother's calico and gingham dresses. "I need more clothes for every day, but we can't buy any dress fabric right now because we had to pay Doctor Cunningham."

"You are taller than your mother was," her father pointed out, "so her dresses will be shorter on you."

"Yes, but they are all floor length, and I detest mopping the floor with my hem."

Her father laughed.

Esther went to her mother's chest of drawers and pulled out the odds-and-ends drawer. "Dad, did you ever wish Mama was a little neater?" she asked, emptying the drawer on the bed between them.

"Sometimes." His smile didn't reach his eyes. "I asked her once why she didn't keep it organized."

"What did she say?"

"She said it was more fun to dig through the pile of stuff to find what she wanted than to have everything lined up and arranged neatly." He smiled again. "Watching her dig through that messy drawer always made me laugh."

He'd been doing some rummaging of his own, and now he held something out to her. "Mama told me she wanted you to have this."

Esther dropped the string of buttons she'd been trying to untangle. Her mother's necklace! It had two interlocking hearts hanging from a delicate silver chain and was one of the few things she had brought with her from her home in South Carolina.

"Mama wanted me to have this?" Esther faltered.

Her father nodded. "She was planning to give it to you next month on your sixteenth birthday."

"Oh, Dad, why did she die?" Esther whispered. "We were all so happy together." A tear slid down her cheek.

Her father's eyes held hers for a long moment. "I don't know why," he said slowly. "And I'm not sure I ever will. But I have to trust God's promise that everything he does is for my eternal good. I can't change what happened, but I *can* change my response to it. Mama told us to go on with our lives, and I can't do that if I'm holding on to the past."

Esther nodded, wiping her eyes before she began sorting the pile of stuff from the drawer. She smoothed the wrinkles in the folded notes and murmured as she worked. "A card from David...a picture of Triangle that he drew when he was ten, a letter that I wrote when I was—It says July, 1856, so that would make me almost twelve."

"Listen," her father said.

Esther heard a team and wagon turn off the road and pull up to their house. "I'll see who it is," she said, getting to her feet.

She opened the door to find Mr. Washburn coming up the porch steps.

"Good morning, Esther," he greeted her cheerfully. "I stopped at the postmaster's in town, and he asked me to drop this off on my way home."

He handed her an envelope. "It's from David, isn't it?"

Esther took one look at the familiar handwriting and beamed at him. "Yes, it is! Thank you for bringing it."

"It was no trouble at all." Mr. Washburn tipped his hat. "Good day." He climbed back into his wagon.

"Say hello to your family for me," Esther called. "And good day to you too."

"I'll tell them," Mr. Washburn promised, clucking to his horses.

"Dad! Mr. Washburn brought us a letter from David," Esther called, closing the door and hurrying into the bedroom.

Her father laid down the paper he'd been reading. "Finally!"

5. Gifts

Esther tore open the envelope and held the letter so she and her father could read at the same time.

Dear Dad and Esther,

I am in Washington, the capital city where President Lincoln lives. It is a fascinating town. A kind farmer let me ride most of the way here in his wagon, so I arrived last night, which was sooner than I'd expected. Esther, I am missing your cooking already. The food you packed for me was gone long ago. I stayed at an inn on the outskirts of town, and they provided my supper and breakfast, but the food doesn't taste like yours. Thanks for the money you sent with me, Dad.

I have been told that the army is camped nearby, so this morning I am setting off to find it. I will write again as soon as I have enlisted and tell you how to address the letters you send to me, so wait to write me until then. In the meantime, try not to forget me.

Lovingly,

David

"It sounds like everything is going well for him." Esther straightened, rubbing her back.

"In spite of the meals."

She laughed. "Him and food! Now I know why he said he would miss me." She tucked the letter back into the envelope.

"I should go make something for lunch." Esther motioned to the things on the bed. "We can finish sorting this later. And I am going to start my own odds-and-ends drawer where I can keep David's letters. Only mine will be neat."

Her father chuckled.

Esther scooped her mother's necklace off the bed and fingered the dainty hearts. "Dad, Mama told me that the first time she wore this was on your wedding day to symbolize your two hearts and lives being united in marriage."

Her father nodded, and she plunged on. "So should I save it to wear on my wedding day? After all, until I get married there won't be two hearts for it to represent."

"Oh, don't worry about that." Her father waved his hand. "Wear it whenever you want. And it *will* represent two hearts. We just don't know who your other heart is yet." He winked at her. "But I'm praying God will bring him along some day."

Esther couldn't help but laugh at his sly grin.

She went to her room and stood in front of her chest of drawers. After emptying the top drawer, she put the letter inside and laid the necklace beside it. She couldn't wear it yet.

Esther plunked a basket of dirty clothes onto the ground beside the well. She glared at the fire under the pot hanging from the tripod. *Can't that wood burn any faster?*

She tucked several unruly strands of hair behind her ear and sighed. Breakfast had been cold because her father was late finishing the chores, she had broken a glass lamp chimney while dusting, and she'd forgotten to put salt in the cornbread for lunch.

"At last!" she exclaimed, feeling that the water in the pot was hot enough. *I hope we hear from David soon,* she thought, pouring the water into a metal washtub. *I need something to brighten up this awful day, and it's been over a week and a half since Mr. Washburn brought us his letter.*

The heavy pot slipped, and Esther gave a little shriek of pain as it hit her arm. She staggered to the fire to hang it back on the tripod and pulled the well bucket toward her, blowing on her arm. After splashing cool well water over the burn, she started scrubbing the clothes on her washboard. Her arm throbbed every time the hot wash water touched it.

Esther wiped tears from her face with her sleeve as she soaped and scrubbed the last pair of trousers.

When the laundry was finally dry, she set up a board to iron on and brought out her mother's two black irons, setting them on a grate several inches above the fire. She always wet the tip of her finger and tested the iron's hot bottom the way her mother had taught her, but she still breathed a sigh of relief each time a dress or shirt was safely ironed.

Then on the last shirt she was so eager to be done that she forgot to test the iron. Her heart sank when she saw the scorch marks, and the tears that she had swallowed came back.

"Oh, Mama! I need you," she sobbed brokenly.

Her arm ached when she bumped her burn, and she cried harder. Feeling a hand on her shoulder, she turned and saw her father.

"Esther, what's the matter?" he asked.

She collapsed against him. "Everything," she choked out, forcing the word past the lump in her throat.

He put his arms around her and rubbed her back while she finished crying. Then he offered her a crumpled handkerchief. She took it gratefully and used the cleanest corner to blow her nose.

"I've been so busy the last couple days," she said in a shaky voice, still leaning against him. "The laundry and cleaning are done now, but the garden is dreadfully full of weeds." She swallowed the lump in her throat. "And I burned my arm."

"I'm sorry, Esther." He squeezed her shoulder. "I'm finished hoeing the corn now, so I can take charge of the garden for you." He gave her an encouraging smile. "If you are done ironing, I'll take these things inside and help you start supper."

Esther smiled as she buttoned her dress the next morning. *Today is my birthday!* She picked up the comb that lay on her chest of drawers and bit her lip, staring at the pretty design carved into the handle. This had been her mother's gift to her last year on her fifteenth birthday.

Mama isn't ever going to be here on my birthday again. With a sigh she twisted her hair into two braids and wrapped them around her head.

"I need to go into town this morning to get some things," her father said during breakfast. "Would you like to go with me?"

Esther swallowed her mouthful of eggs and glanced up at him.

"I thought we could do something fun together since it's your birthday," he added, and her face brightened.

"That would be nice, but I need to make a batch of bread after breakfast. I should have made it yesterday, but I didn't have time."

He shrugged. "Then we can do something when I get back. All right?"

Esther nodded. She sang as she washed the dishes, made the bread dough, and started a fire in their box stove to bake the rounded loaves.

When her father drove in the lane and stopped Triangle beside the porch, she ran out to help him carry his purchases inside.

"Hello, happy daughter of mine," he greeted her with a grin. "Did your bread bake well?"

"Yes, it did." Esther flashed him a smile and leaned over the side of the wagon, filling her arms with packages and carrying them inside.

She helped him unharness Triangle and put her in the pasture, and then they sat down at the dining room table where they had deposited everything from town. Beside the regular food and supplies, there was a glass chimney to replace the one she had broken.

"This is for your birthday." Her father handed her a package. "I know it's been hard for you to manage the house and garden by yourself, but you are doing a wonderful job."

"Thank you." Esther tore off the paper. "A new book!" she exclaimed, beaming at him. "I can't wait to read it." She ran her fingers over the title on the spine. "*Highland Rose.* Thank you, Dad."

"That isn't all." He held up a finger. "I have another letter from David."

Pulling an envelope from his pocket, he took out the letter and read the first line aloud. "Dear Dad and Esther."

His eyes scanned the page. "Oh!" He stood up, and his chair fell over backward. "I almost *did* forget.

"Here, Esther, you can go ahead and read this. I'll be back in a minute." He righted his chair and rushed up the stairs.

Forget what? Esther smoothed out the letter and started in where he had left off.

I enlisted a week ago. When I finally found the place, I saw them turning some fellows away, so I wondered if they would take me. But they only turned away boys who were too young or who failed to pass the doctor's inspection. I am not sure what the doctor was inspecting us for, but anyone who was under eighteen was considered too young. At least, that is probably what the regulations say. There are a lot of fellows in my company who are under eighteen, I am sure. Some have even told me so, and they brag about how they blustered their way past the recruiting officer.

Despite all that, I am glad I landed in the company I did. I have met most of the men in the short time I've been with them, and I have the best captain a soldier could wish for. His name is Daniel Armstrong, and we have already become friends. He is only two years older than I am, but he organized his own small company. Even though several of his men are older than he is, they all respect him because he is considerate to everyone.

The fire I am sitting beside is dying, and I should turn in for the night. I have to get up even earlier here than I did at home—for roll call.

And, Dad, do not forget about the twenty-third. You can write to me now. Address your letters to Pvt. David Sullivan, and then add the information on this envelope about my company, regiment, and so on.

Impatiently waiting to hear from you,

David

Esther finished reading the letter as her father came downstairs and stood beside her.

He smiled and handed her a package. "Before David left, he wrapped this up and asked me to give it to you on your birthday. I'll read his letter while you open it."

Esther tore the brown paper from the flat, rectangular package, surprised that her brother had actually gone to the trouble of wrapping his gift.

She sucked in a quick breath. "Oh, how beautiful!"

Carved across the bottom of a large wooden plaque was the word, "Triangle," and above that was the outline of a rearing horse. The wood around the upper half of its body was chiseled down and sanded smooth. Esther ran her fingers over the flailing hooves, the pricked ears, and the flowing mane. But its hindquarters, long tail, and hind legs were still little more than a rough sketch.

"It isn't finished," she said, looking up at her father.

"Read the note," he said without taking his eyes off the letter. Esther lifted the plaque and found a folded piece of paper.

Dear Esther,

I hope you like this carving of Triangle. Mama helped me with the lettering. I know it looks a little strange now, but I will finish it as soon as I can. I will miss you while I am gone, and I wish you a happy birthday.

Your brother,

David.

"It's magnificent, even if it isn't finished." Esther turned to her father, who was chuckling over the end of David's letter. "I didn't know he could carve like this."

"That's because he wanted the plaque to be a surprise for you. He's been working on it for a long time."

"Then it will probably be even longer until it's finished." Esther sighed. "He seems pretty taken with his new company and captain."

Her father grinned. "I think company life will be good for him. His captain sounds like a decent fellow, and hopefully the rest of the men are too. But I am sure he'll get a leave and come home to see us before too long."

Esther took her gifts and the letters upstairs to put them away before she started on lunch. She set the plaque beside her wash basin and put *Highland Rose* on her bed, hoping she would have time to read it that afternoon.

Opening her top drawer, she reread David's letters and the note before putting them away. *I don't care how good company life may be for you, David,* she thought. *I miss you.*

6. Heroes

The next day, Esther wrote to David.

Dear David,

The carving of Triangle is amazing, even though it isn't finished. You captured that one fascinating moment at the end of all your "Paul Revere" rides when she rears for you. How long were you working on it? I had no idea you were carving anything.

Remember all those secret things we used to do together? Like wading in the creek after we grew tired of hoeing corn, spying on the Washburns when they had company, and swinging from the rafters in the haymow? Remember how devastated we were when Mama found out, one mischievous deed at a time, and told Dad? It still makes me laugh to think about it.

The garden is still producing, but I'm done harvesting the beans now. I have been very busy, and sometimes I feel overwhelmed by my responsibilities. Dad helps me as much as he can, though, and we are managing. It is so much quieter here without you, David.

Moses Pritchard, Joshua's little brother, broke his arm last Thursday. He was showing it off at church and using it as an excuse to make the other boys do things for him. He told them some nonsense about how brave he'd been, but his sister Lily told everyone the truth—that he'd cried and screamed when Doctor Cunningham set the bone.

There was a sewing bee at the Washburns' house last week. I left some sandwiches here for Dad's lunch and was over there all day. Most of the women from town were there, and we made sheets and bandages to send to the hospitals full of wounded men. Mrs. Pritchard is traveling down to Manassas Junction to visit her sister on Tuesday next, so she has been commissioned to deliver them.

It was fun to get out and do something other than regular housework for a change, but I was upset to hear the women argue over their different views on the war. How can we ever hope to win this war if we don't put aside our differences and work together, side by side?

I also found out that we are not the only ones with relatives in the South. I don't like to think about fighting against our own relatives, and we don't even know them. It must be terrible for the people who are close to their relatives to find themselves on opposite sides now.

In his answering letter, David wrote:

I must say, Esther, you are altogether too pessimistic. If you could be in camp with me for even just one day, you would realize that we are working together. Being here with the men has taught me that more than anything else could have. They are all my buddies and, despite what we say in our quarrels, we would give our lives for each other if the need arose. My captain, Daniel, is like an older brother to me, and he enjoys teaching me things. I really look up to him, because even when he's upset, he doesn't belittle us men, like I've seen other officers do in their companies.

I know what you mean about people fighting against their own relatives. There is a man in my company who grew up in the South but moved up North to marry a girl eleven years ago. I had thought that all Southerners upheld slavery, even if they didn't own slaves, but after meeting Lewis, I know that isn't true. His father and brothers never supported slavery either. Lewis had tears in his eyes when he told me that he enlisted to keep his wife and children from being ostracized as Southern sympathizers.

I am glad you liked the carving of Triangle. I started it last summer, hoping to have it done in time for your fifteenth birthday, but I didn't know how hard it would be. Like I said, I will finish it as soon as I can. Maybe when I come home on leave or when the war is over and I come home for good. But what did you mean by my "Paul Revere" rides? I couldn't figure that out.

You made it sound like we did all those secret things together when we were younger, and (your memory must be failing) that isn't quite true. I was the one swinging from the rafters in the haymow, while you sat in the safety of the hay, watching.

Good-bye for now. Tell Dad that I am behaving even though he isn't here to make me.

Esther smiled at this, and when she read it to her father, he chuckled. To answer David's question about her description of his rides on Triangle, she wrote:

When you were thirteen Paul Revere was your hero, and you said that someday you would be as famous as he is.

You would gallop Triangle around the pasture, pretending that you were warning the citizens of Lexington and Concord, Massachusetts, and you made her rear at the climax of all your "spectacular" rides. Since you didn't remember your Paul Revere rides, I think you are the one with the failing memory.

David's next letter said:

Let's drop the charges of the failing memory on both sides, Esther. All right? Now that you have mentioned it, I do remember the time when Paul Revere was my hero, but he isn't anymore. My hero is my captain, Daniel Armstrong

After nearly a dozen letters had passed between them, David remarked:

We have been in training ever since I enlisted, but it has been getting harder of late. The officers had told us a while ago that the most rigorous training was still ahead of us, and they were right. I really do not see the purpose of the strict routines and schedules they hold us to and the relentless drilling. We have to practice marching in formation, loading our guns quickly, and learning how to respond to all the different commands for hours on end. It is so monotonous, and I do not see how it is going to help us win the war. A little is not too bad—even necessary, I admit—but it has been almost four months since I enlisted, and I haven't even seen a Rebel soldier yet. All I have done is drill, drill, and drill some more.

When Esther read David's opinion of the training and endless drills to her father, he chuckled. "For all his complaining, I would say it will take more than physical labor to dampen the spirits of those men. The routines and drilling will help them become a better company."

In her next letter, Esther wrote:

> Dad thinks all that training is good for you, David. Besides, you can't quit now, can you? How long did you sign up for?
>
> It snowed yesterday for the first time. The first time this year that it has actually stuck to the ground, I mean. It isn't very much, but there was enough for me to make a snowball to throw at Dad when I was helping him with chores this morning.
>
> I have noticed our roosters fighting more often lately, and last night when I was feeding them, the older one attacked me, pecking my arm. My long sleeves protected me, but the second time he flew at me he scratched my hand. Horrible bird! Dad chopped off his head this morning, and we are going to eat him for supper. I invited the Washburns over, and we shall rejoice in the demise of the wicked fowl.
>
> I was wondering what you and all the men in the army are going to do this winter when it gets snowy and blowy. Won't you get cold in your tents? Or do you get to come home for the winter? That would be nice! Dad and I really miss you.

She waited eagerly for David's reply, and when it came, she tore open the envelope and unfolded the letter.

Dear Esther,

I signed up for one year, and no matter what Dad thinks about my endless training, I am still tired of it. We have gotten a break from it the last couple weeks, though,

because we've had to build lots of little cabins for our winter camp. They will be warmer than tents, not only because
they shield us from the wind and can be heated, but also
because we are squished into them like potatoes in a bin.

So, no, I do not get to come home for the winter, but yesterday I received permission to come home for Christmas!
Of course, all the fellows want to go home for Christmas,
but they cannot let everyone leave at the same time. I
will actually be coming home in about a week, because
I am one of the lucky fellows who get to have an early
Christmas. You don't mind having it a couple weeks early,
do you? If you really miss me as much as I miss you, I am
sure we will have the best Christmas ever.

He had written more, but Esther couldn't wait to tell her
father the good news. He had given her the letter and gone outside to start the evening chores. She grabbed her shawl and ran
after him.

"Dad!" she called, rushing through the barn to where he was
milking Milksop. "David is coming home in a week for an early
Christmas! Isn't that wonderful?"

The milk stopped splish-splashing into the pail as her father
looked up, a wide grin spreading over his face. "He is finally tearing himself away from that remarkable company and that *wonderful* captain of his? That is indeed very good news."

Esther laughed and twirled, narrowly missing a post. "I can
hardly wait!"

7. A First Lieutenant

Esther winced, stretching from her cramped position at the wash-tub. *I mustn't ever wait so long to do the washing again,* she thought.

Although David hadn't written the exact date he would get home, her father said they shouldn't expect him for several more days, since he would have to walk or catch a ride the whole way.

I am sure he will get here as fast as he can, even if he does have to walk, Esther told herself optimistically. *Maybe he will even get here tomorrow.*

She hummed a cheerful ditty as she finished scrubbing the clothes. There was a movement at her collar, and she felt warm water trickling down her back. She yelped, shuddering as she scrambled to her feet and whirled around.

There stood her brother, rubbing his hands on his trousers and chuckling.

"David!" she cried, launching herself at him and wrapping her arms around his neck. "Oh, you cannot imagine how much I've missed you."

David hugged her back, spinning her in a half circle. "Yes, I can, Little Birdie," he whispered. Then he added in his usual, lighthearted voice, "I've missed you too."

He released her, and she stepped back to take in his dark-blue uniform and matching cap. The wet spots on his trousers where he'd dried his hands reminded her of the wet place at the back of her neck. She rubbed it vigorously.

"Was that dirty water from my washtub?" she demanded, frowning at him. "I see you haven't changed much."

David's grin widened, and he chuckled again. "Sorry," he apologized, making a small bow, "but when I saw you bending over that tub, I couldn't resist."

Esther opened her mouth to scold him, but the little bars on the shoulders of his uniform caught her attention. "What does this mean?" she asked instead, touching the gold stripe on one of the bars.

An unfamiliar voice behind her said, "It means he is a first lieutenant."

Esther swung around. A young man stood just inside the kitchen doorway wearing the same dark-blue uniform as her brother. She looked back at David and raised her eyebrows. He stepped up beside her.

"Esther, this is Captain Daniel Armstrong. Daniel"—he turned to the young man—"this is my sister, Esther."

Captain Daniel Armstrong took off his cap and dipped his head with a warm smile.

Esther curtsied and offered him a friendly smile of her own.

"I am pleased to meet you, Miss Sullivan," Captain Armstrong said. "Your brother talked about you often."

"As often as he wrote to us about you?" Esther grinned at David and then at Captain Armstrong. "Please, just call me Esther."

David's captain nodded. "All right."

"Have you seen Dad yet?" Esther turned back to her brother. "He's in the barn."

"Yes, I saw him," David said. "We went to the barn first, because we had to put Daniel's horse, Raven, away. We rode double the whole way, which is why we arrived sooner than you expected."

"Sooner than I expected is right." Esther tried to brush a curl out of her face, suddenly feeling nervous and a little embarrassed by all the washing lying around. "I'm so glad you are home, David, but supper might be later than usual."

"Make something extra good—I'm starved for your cooking." David grinned. "Would you like us to empty these tubs of water for you before I show Daniel around?"

"That would be lovely." Esther gave him a grateful smile. "Thank you, David."

He turned to his captain, but Daniel had already plunked his cap on his brown hair and grabbed a tub handle. Esther smirked as David copied him. Their blue uniforms made them look much the same, except Daniel was nearly a head taller than David.

A few minutes later, the door opened, and Esther heard someone stamping their feet. Thinking it was David and his friend, she called out, "Thank you for emptying the tubs for me!"

Her father said, "You're welcome," and gave a mirthful little chuckle.

"Dad!" Esther stepped into the dining room. "I thought—"

David thundered down the stairs with Daniel close behind him. "Hello again, Dad!" he exclaimed.

The men went into the living room, and Esther went back into the kitchen. Using her mother's recipes, she made herbed potatoes with butter and a sweet sauce to drizzle over the side of ham she warmed up. Setting the table with her mother's good china, she carried out the bread, butter, and currant jelly.

"Supper is ready," she announced.

The men stopped talking, and David sprang up from the sofa. "It sure smells good!"

Everyone was seated at the table when Esther returned from fetching the potatoes. Her father and David were in their usual places, but as she set the bowl down she saw that Daniel was sitting in her mother's chair.

Memories flooded her mind, bringing a quick rush of tears to her eyes. She didn't realize she was staring at Daniel until he glanced up at her.

Embarrassed, she hurried into the kitchen. Leaning against the wooden worktable, she whispered, "I miss you, Mama." Her voice broke, and several tears rolled down her cheeks.

Taking a deep breath, she removed her apron and wiped her face. Picking up the platter of ham, she headed back to the dining room. They were laughing about something when she came in, and she hoped no one had noticed her tears.

But after her father prayed for the food, David caught her gaze and said softly, "Supper looks great, Little Birdie."

He noticed, she thought, but his compliment lightened her heart. "Thank you," she said with a smile.

Daniel glanced at her brother. "What did you call her, David? Or shouldn't I ask?"

David started buttering his slice of bread. "Little Birdie?" he repeated. "It's just my nickname for Esther." He turned to her. "Do you remember when I started calling you that?"

"Barely. I think I was almost four. Mama was spooning me in, and you said I looked like a little bird begging worms from its mother."

David smirked. "Actually, I said you looked like a scraggly little bird."

Her father laughed. "David, stop teasing your sister and tell me how you became a first lieutenant. I thought you had to work your way up."

"Usually you do, unless you get chosen the way I did." David smiled at his captain. "The first lieutenant, William Cooper, caught scarlet fever on leave, and it left him blind. So Daniel appointed me as his first lieutenant."

"Was there a particular reason you chose David?" Esther's father inquired.

Daniel set down his half-eaten slice of bread. "He is well liked by the men. They usually follow his suggestions before there's even a need for an order. I feel more comfortable leaving him in charge than anyone else, because he held the men together when I was busy even before it was his job as first lieutenant."

"That's good to hear! So who is in charge now, since both of you are gone?"

David and his captain exchanged knowing looks. "Adam Goodlow, the second lieutenant," Daniel said. "I'm going to cut my leave short, because if I can catch him neglecting his duties like I suspect he will be, I can take disciplinary measures."

Esther fetched the pudding cake she had made that morning from the kitchen.

"That looks good, Esther. Here, I'll take some."

"Are you sure you still have room for it in your stomach?" Esther handed the dish to her brother.

"Of course I have room for it." David took a large portion. "It's been almost forever since I've had some of your pudding cake."

"Or any cake," Daniel muttered, also taking a large portion.

Any cake? Esther's eyes widened.

"Will you spend the rest of your leave here, or are you planning to go somewhere else?" Esther's father asked as Daniel passed him the dessert. "You are welcome to stay with us as long as you like."

"He's on his way to his brother's in Ohio," David volunteered, his mouth full of cake.

Esther raised her eyebrows at his lack of manners, and he ducked his head with an apologetic grin.

"Ethan's the only family I have left," Daniel said. "I told him I would come and spend several days with him and Molly and the children."

"You never told me your brother had a family," David said.

"You never asked," Daniel retorted good-naturedly. "They had three children when they moved to Ohio, and I know they've had at least one more since. Maybe two."

"Sounds like it's been a while since you saw them," Esther's father commented.

Esther stopped eating. "But if you go back early, doesn't that mean David has to also?"

Captain Armstrong was silent for a moment. "Yes, unless he wants to walk back. Would you be willing to go back early with me?" he asked David.

"I don't know." David glanced at his father. "When are you planning to leave for your brother's place?" he asked.

"If you can spare an empty corner for me, I was hoping to stay here tonight and leave in the morning," Daniel said.

David sighed with relief. "Of course you may stay. Then I'll have until tomorrow morning to decide."

"All right. You are all excused." Esther's father stood up.

"Thank you for the delicious meal, Esther," Daniel said.

Esther smiled and began to clear the table. "You're welcome."

David and Daniel went out to help her father with the chores, but they came back in before she had finished washing the dishes. Daniel offered to wipe the dining room table, and when he'd left the kitchen, Esther turned to her brother.

"David, where did he get that scar?" she asked quietly.

"What scar?" David's face was blank.

"It's just above his right eyebrow." Esther touched her own forehead. "I noticed it this afternoon when you introduced him."

"Oh, yes, that scar." David shrugged. "I don't know."

"Daniel, where did you get your scar?" he asked as soon as his friend came back into the kitchen.

"My scar?" Daniel rubbed the little white mark. "It's a self-inflicted wound." He smirked. "I was trying to carve something with the wrong side of my knife when I was nine."

David chuckled. "I've done that before." He turned to Esther. "Where is that carving of Triangle I gave you?"

"Upstairs." Esther fetched the plaque from her room.

"That is good!" Daniel exclaimed when she showed it to him. "Much more detailed than anything I've ever done."

8. Early Christmas

"What is your decision, David?" Esther's father asked during breakfast the next morning. "Are you going to let this young upstart of a captain take you away from us before it is absolutely necessary?" His eyes twinkled.

David polished off his second helping of fresh biscuits and sausage gravy. "If Daniel wants to swing by here on his way to headquarters and pick me up, that would be nice. Riding with him will be faster than walking, so it will actually give me more time with you." He smiled at Esther.

"Sounds good." Esther's father stood up. "I'm going out to do the chores. Thank you for breakfast, Esther. It was delicious."

"Yes, it was," David and Daniel agreed. "Thank you."

"You're welcome," Esther said.

"See you next week," Daniel called as he and David went out to the barn.

Esther waved when he rode past the kitchen window on his black horse, and he waved back, flashing her a smile.

"Let's go ahead and celebrate tonight as Christmas Eve," Esther's father suggested while they were eating lunch. "Is that all right with both of you?"

"It's fine with me," David said quickly. "I'm not sure I can wait much longer."

Esther grinned. "That is precisely what I was thinking."

So that night they hung their stockings on the mantel in the living room. The next morning it was still dark when Esther felt someone shake her shoulder. She kept her eyes closed and listened to her brother's whispered entreaties.

"Please, Esther, wake up. Come on, open your eyes and roll out of bed. Please...wake...up."

When she didn't move, he said severely, "If you want to go down with me, you better get up now. I'm not waiting any longer."

"But it isn't even light yet," Esther protested, shoving back her quilt and sliding out of bed. "Couldn't you have slept a little longer?" She followed him down the stairs.

"Not on Christmas morning." David skipped the creaky fourth step and rushed into the living room. He uncovered the coals in the fireplace and added wood.

"Oh, David. Look!" Esther saw a package on the sofa with her name on it and tore it open. "Such pretty cloth!" She held it up against herself and twirled, her dark braids flying.

"Do you like it?" David grinned, the lines in his forehead relaxing.

"Is it from you?" Esther asked, and when he nodded, she gave him a big hug. "Thank you, David. It's beautiful!"

They both pulled down their woolen stockings and sat in front of the fire. Esther emptied hers into her lap and remembered last

Christmas. Her mother had been sitting here with them, going through her own stocking.

Esther looked over to where her brother was inspecting his treasures in the firelight. "David," she whispered, trying to swallow the lump in her throat. "I wish Mama was here."

David turned to look at her, his eyes softening. After a moment he said huskily, "So do I."

She scooted closer to him and laid her head on his shoulder, drawing a shaky breath as a tear dropped onto his shirt. He put his arm around her, and they sat in silence, staring into the flickering orange flames.

Esther had more fun that week than she'd had since her mother died. She had missed her optimistic, dry-humored brother more than she realized.

After the morning service at church on Sunday, they went over to the Washburns for lunch and the afternoon. Esther played with their baby Margaret and took a short walk with Lydia.

That evening while her father and brother discussed the war and all the other latest news, Esther read *Highland Rose* again. It was about a young girl in Scotland who lived with a poor family who loved her. On her eighteenth birthday, she discovered that she had high-class relatives and was to inherit a magnificent castle, but she chose to stay with the family who'd raised her.

Esther sighed and smiled a little as she read the last sentence. "Adam Myrtle," she murmured, looking at the author's name, "you wrote an amazing story."

"Who are you talking to?" David scooted over from the other end of the sofa as his father put more wood on the fire.

Esther slammed the book shut. "Myself."

"Is that a new book?" He reached out and tipped it so he could see the title. "I don't think I've seen it before."

She nodded and handed it to him. "Dad gave it to me on my birthday."

"Do you like it?"

Esther grinned. "Yes. The family in it, the MacDonalds, reminds me of the Washburns."

David started flipping through the book. "I could never read all this." He slammed the book shut even harder than she had, and she laughed.

It warmed up outside one day, and David rode Triangle. After he did the rearing finale, Esther rode for a while.

When she dismounted, she patted the brown mare. "Good girl, Triangle."

Then she grinned mischievously at her brother. "Should I pat you too?" She patted his arm. "Thanks for letting me ride, David."

He grunted. "Oh, go on."

In the evenings while their father read from the Bible or they all talked, Esther knitted and David worked on his carving of Triangle.

"Oh, bother!" he exclaimed one evening, hitting his forehead. "I broke it!"

Esther gathered up her knitting and looked over his shoulder. His knife had gouged a slice off the horse's belly. "You didn't break it, David," she consoled him. "You did mess it up a little, but it doesn't matter. I still like it."

David sighed, rubbing his fingers over the uneven edge.

By the time his leave was up, he had finished carving all of it except the part below the horse's hocks.

"I expect Daniel will show up sometime today," David said one morning as he marched down the steps, tucking in his shirt. "I was almost afraid he would come yesterday."

Esther heard a knock on the door as she was making lunch. She wiped her hands on her apron and opened the door to find Daniel Armstrong on the porch.

He took off his hat and swept her a bow. "Good day, Esther."

She stepped back. "Do come in, Captain Armstrong."

"Thank you." He stepped inside. "And you can just call me Daniel, if you want."

She nodded. "I think David is in his room," she said, motioning to the stairs. "He thought you might come today, but you can probably still surprise him."

Daniel grinned. "I'll see what I can do."

He went upstairs, and Esther returned to the kitchen. She figured Daniel would want to leave right away, so she packed a basket of food and carried it to the dining room.

David came down the stairs with his haversack slung over one shoulder.

Esther hugged him. "Good-bye, David. Write to us when you can."

He reached for the unruly strand of hair hanging in her face and tucked it behind her ear. "I will. And I'll expect to hear from you too."

Esther squeezed his hand. "I'll write you lots of letters, I promise." She handed the basket to Daniel. "I made some sandwiches for you."

Daniel's face lit up. "Thank you, Esther. For the sandwiches and your hospitality last week."

Esther smiled. "You're welcome. Good-bye."

They went out, David trying to peek into the basket, and Daniel swinging it out of his reach.

"Good-bye, Esther," David called, grabbing Daniel's shoulder and shoving him sideways.

"Behave or I'll make you walk," Daniel threatened, swinging onto his black horse and cantering toward the road.

David dashed out the lane after Raven, and Esther grinned as she closed the door.

9. Socks and Cookies

David's first letter came a couple weeks after he had returned to the army.

> Daniel was right about Adam, the second lieutenant. When we returned our camp was a mess, and the men were running wild. The sergeant, Jack Mason, is second lieutenant now. He is a cheerful person, which is nice, because we are all restless and tired of doing nothing.
>
> Several of the companies in our regiment have put on short plays as a diversion for the rest of us. Daniel, Mason, and I persuaded our men to help us act out an imaginary meeting between President Lincoln and the Rebel leader, Jefferson Davis. We used our tallest private for President Lincoln and our shortest one for Jefferson Davis. Mason

> planned what they would say to each other, and the rest of us divided ourselves between them for their separate armies. I couldn't stop laughing while the president and Davis were going at it, so it's fortunate that I didn't have an important role.
>
> We all take turns cooking up our rations, but there are half a dozen men in our company who can cook better than the rest of us, so they do it the most. Cook better simply means burn the biscuits brown instead of black, and although I am exaggerating a little, some of these rations really are not fit to eat.

Esther laughed at this until she remembered what he and Daniel had said about her cake. With her next letter she sent a package of several pairs of knitted socks and a few dozen cookies. David's answering letter came quickly.

> Little Birdie, those cookies you sent were delicious! I shared them—and the socks—with the men, and they have been saying you are an angel straight from heaven.

Esther smiled at this compliment and sent several more batches of cookies.

Spring came, and Esther planted the garden. Her father often plowed in the field from dawn till dusk, and she carried sandwiches and tea out to him.

One afternoon late in April, David rode in their lane on Daniel's black horse, Raven. Daniel had let him use the horse to shorten his traveling time. As they ate supper, David told them how the Potomac Army's General McClellan had taken the Union troops to the Virginia Peninsula and now occupied Yorktown.

"We marched up the York River toward Richmond all last week," he said, reaching for more bread. "Esther, this bread is so good. I am sick of eating hardtack."

Esther smiled and passed him the butter.

During the four days David was at home, he spent nearly all his time in the field with her father, helping with the spring planting. No matter how sick he was of eating hardtack, Esther could tell he was eager to get back to the army.

After returning to his regiment, David wrote of renewed drills and then skirmishes with the Confederate Army. Esther told him she worried more now, but he said his company hadn't been in any heavy fighting yet.

Late in August Esther's father came home from town with another letter from David.

"At last!" Esther exclaimed in relief, ripping open the envelope. "It's been more than a month since we heard from him."

She held the letter so they could both read at the same time.

Dear Dad and Esther,

I'm sorry for not writing sooner. My company was split up during the skirmishes and battles three weeks ago, but we are finally all together again.

Nothing is normal around here anymore. We are moving from place to place, constantly suspecting confrontation from the Rebels, always being warned to be prepared for another battle, and so on. Living under such conditions is quite a strain on a fellow's nerves. The battles I have been in were terrible, nothing short of nightmarish experiences, and I am not looking forward to any more.

Esther looked at her father, and he squeezed her shoulder. She prayed more for her brother that night and for the next several weeks. Once when she couldn't sleep, she looked out her window and saw her father kneeling next to the big rock at the edge of the woods.

Around the middle of September, Mr. Washburn drove in the lane with his team and wagon. Before long Esther heard the wagon leave and her father come inside.

"What did Mr. Washburn want?" Esther called.

He came into the kitchen and stopped behind her. "He was in town today, shoeing his team, and he saw the list of casualties and such for the Second Battle of Bull Run."

"Yes, you told me a couple weeks ago that the North lost that battle." Esther turned and searched his tense face, her stomach twisting.

"Daddy," she whispered, stepping toward him, "was David killed?"

"No, Esther." Her father touched her cheek. "He's listed as wounded in action."

Esther stared at him, envisioning David sprawled on the battlefield or lying in a hospital bed minus an arm or leg. "We have to go bring him home, Dad," she announced, her voice rising. "There can't be enough doctors and nurses to go around, but if we bring him home, Dr. Cunningham will help us take care of him. We could borrow the Washburns' team and wagon, and I am sure they would do our chores while we're gone."

"Esther." Her father took hold of her shoulders. "David is way down in Manassas, Virginia, and we would have to drive through Sharpsburg, Maryland, to get there. Our army fought a major battle with the Confederates at Sharpsburg just four days ago."

She studied his face. "Who won? Is the Confederate army still there?"

"We won. General Lee and his army retreated."

"We would be safe then, right? Please, I just want David to be home." She rocked on her heels and tipped her head. "Please, Daddy?"

He held her gaze for a moment, and his expression softened. "All right. We'll go get him. I'll talk to the Washburns if you pack what we'll need to take along. Should we try to leave tomorrow?"

Esther nodded, smiling. "I'll be ready," she promised.

For the rest of that day she made food, packed clothes and bedding, and put the house in order.

"You can take Triangle and Milksop over to the Washburns' pasture tonight," her father said while they were eating supper. "Mr. Washburn said he'd send Peter over tomorrow morning with the team and wagon." He leaned back in his chair. "There. I have accomplished my part of the bargain."

"I'll finish my part too," Esther assured him. "Don't look so smug."

He chuckled.

Esther was finishing the breakfast dishes the next morning when she heard hoof beats coming in the lane. She glanced out the window and hurried outside, drying her hands on her apron. "Dad! Peter is here."

Sixteen-year-old Peter Washburn helped them load their things into the wagon. "You are so fortunate to be going to Manassas," he told Esther. "I wish I could see the place where two battles were fought. I've always wanted to see the army." He sighed.

Esther rolled her eyes. "I doubt the army is still there. All we will see are hurt and wounded men who probably wish the army never existed. Besides, our army lost both battles."

He was quiet then, but when he was walking around the field on his way home, he called, "You'll see. We'll win this war and show those Rebels a thing or two."

Esther rolled her eyes again at his cockiness.

Her father came out of the house with the Bible and stowed it under the wagon seat beside the food hampers and folded quilts. He looked at her and nodded. "I think we have everything."

"Then let's go." Esther scrambled up to the wagon seat.

Her father climbed up and sat beside her, clucking to the horses.

"Daddy, do you know how to get there?" Esther asked as they drove through Kirksville.

"Do you think that would help?" He turned to look at her with an innocent expression and then chuckled. "I know we have to go east to Chambersburg before we head south, but we will have to stop and ask for directions after that."

The trees around Sharpsburg had been splintered by exploding shells, and when they drove through it, Esther saw muskets, bayonets, and soldiers' belongings still littering the ground. She stared in horror at several wounded men on the street.

It's been over a week since the battle! Is this what happened to David?

Sorrow flooded her as she thought of the soldiers' families. She sniffed, swallowing the lump in her throat. "Isn't it awful, Daddy? So many families will never see their men again."

Her father nodded. "War is horrible. David wanted to get in on the excitement, but this is what ends up happening."

Esther sniffed again, rubbing her nose with the back of her hand. *I want to find him so badly,* she thought.

10. Centreville, Virginia

Even though the nights were a little cool, the weather was pleasant for the entire trip. The trees, flashing the brilliant reds and oranges of autumn, made the scenery gorgeous. They stopped to ask for directions several times, and it only took them ten days to reach Manassas Junction. Esther's father halted the team in front of the makeshift hospital and handed her the reins.

"Can't I come in?" she asked when he jumped to the ground and started for the door.

"If there's any chance David is here, then you can come in and help me look for him."

Esther slumped back on the seat and fidgeted with the reins until her father returned. "Isn't David here?" she asked as he climbed back on the wagon.

"No." He took the reins and clucked to the horses. "We'll try Centreville, a little town several miles northeast of here."

"Oh." Esther grabbed the side of the seat as the wagon jounced through a pothole.

In Centreville, they found the brick building that served as a hospital. Esther hopped down off the wagon while her father tied the team to a tree, and they went inside together. Her father left to speak to a doctor who was hurrying past, and Esther stared at the wounded men around her. A few stared back, but most looked either asleep or unconscious. She swallowed hard and started walking between the beds, anxious to find David.

He wasn't in the first room she searched, or the second. There was a sign over the next doorway she came to.

"Room four," she muttered, starting up the first aisle.

Then she saw him, and her heart did a little flip-flop.

Her brother's left shoulder was wrapped up, and his left leg was bandaged and strapped to a board. He was reading a piece of paper, but when she stopped at the foot of his bed, he looked up and met her eyes.

They stared at each other. "Esther?" David whispered. "What are you doing here?" He held out his right hand, and the paper fell to the floor.

Esther smiled, relief flooding through her at the sound of his voice. She sat on the edge of his bed and squeezed his hand. "Dad and I came to take you home."

"Home?" David relaxed and then suddenly tensed. "No! I can't go home."

The despair in his voice surprised Esther, but before she could say anything, she heard footsteps and turned to see her father.

"Dad?" David shifted his good leg. "Dad, I was wrong." His voice trembled.

Esther's father sat down on the other side of the bed. "That doesn't matter anymore, David," he said gently. "We're taking you home."

David shook his head. "You don't want me."

Esther's eyes widened. "Of course we do, David."

"You don't know what I've done."

Esther looked at her father. "What have you done?" he asked David quietly.

A muscle in David's jaw tightened. "I-I killed a man."

"*A* man?" Hoarse laughter came from the bed beside David's. "You've killed more than one, Sullivan."

Esther turned to glare at the bearded, middle-aged man.

He stopped laughing and shrugged. "I was one of the men in his company," he said, motioning to David. "He was a good soldier. Just got his discharge papers a minute ago."

Beside Esther, David stirred. "Carter, keep out of this, will you?"

The man saluted. "Yes sir, Lieutenant." He turned his face away.

"David," Esther's father said softly. "No matter what happened, we still love you, and we're going to take you home. You concentrate on getting well, and we'll talk later. All right?"

David nodded, letting out a long breath. "Thanks, Dad."

"What happened, David?" Esther motioned to his shoulder and leg.

David shifted, wincing. "It was an exploding shell."

"Same shell that took off my leg," Carter spoke up.

Esther looked over at him. His face was still turned away from them.

"Carter," David warned.

"I'm out of it," Carter said quickly, hunching his shoulders.

"A fragment of exploding shell hit my shoulder," David explained, "and another piece broke my leg. The doctor here set my leg and wrapped my shoulder, but it's been a while since he checked on me."

"I'll take care of you now, David." Esther brushed a sweaty black curl off his forehead. "You have a fever," she murmured.

She gave her father the discharge paper David had dropped, and he slid it into his pocket as he stood up. "We're going to go talk to the doctor, David, but we'll be back."

David closed his eyes. "I'm not going anywhere."

The doctor was in another room dressing a soldier's wound. He glanced up as Esther and her father approached. "What can I do for you?" Although he looked tired, his voice was pleasant.

Esther's father hesitated a moment. "I would like your opinion on my son's condition. David Sullivan, room four, bed twenty-three."

"Is he the one you asked me about before?" The doctor pinched the bridge of his nose. "Let's see…" He removed his spectacles and rubbed them on his dirty white coat.

"Or some advice," Esther's father added. "You see, we came to take him home, and I was wondering how the trip would affect his wounds."

"His shoulder is almost healed, although he won't be able to use that arm properly anymore. But it's his leg I'm worried…"

The doctor trailed off suddenly. "Trip?" he echoed. Replacing his spectacles, he glanced at Esther and then eyed her father. "You can't take him anywhere," he said. "He is wounded and must not be moved. I know we don't have enough nurses to go around, but he's in the hospital where he belongs."

"I can take care of him at home," Esther said quickly.

The doctor turned to her. "Have you ever dressed a wound?"

"No." Esther met his gaze without flinching. "But I can learn."

He studied her for a moment, and some of the weariness left his eyes. "All right then, you can be my assistant for the rest of the day. I'll decide in the morning whether or not you can take your brother home."

Esther glanced at her father. *I guess it won't hurt us to wait till morning,* she thought.

The doctor motioned to the bed beside him. "This fellow had his leg amputated a week ago, and it's time for the bandage to be changed. Ask him how he's doing while I get clean water." He picked up a basin from the floor and walked away.

Esther turned to the young man in the bed, suddenly feeling small and scared. But she forgot about herself when she looked at his face and realized he couldn't be much older than she was. *I can't imagine living without a leg!*

"Good afternoon!" She smiled at him. "I am Esther Sullivan. My father and I came here to get my brother."

The young man nodded. "I heard your talk with the doctor. Pleased to meet you." He glanced at her father.

"Richard Sullivan." Esther's father reached out to shake the young man's hand. "And you are?"

"My ma named me Philip Stephen, but everyone calls me Stephen," the young man said. "Stephen McArthur."

He leaned forward. "Don't let the doctor discourage you. Doctors are all right—in fact, I probably wouldn't be alive without them—but I'd much rather be home with my family and sweetheart."

"Don't worry." Esther lifted her chin. "We're not leaving without David."

Stephen smiled. "He's lucky to have you two looking out for him."

The doctor returned, his basin filled with clean water. Strips of cloth were draped over his arm. He set down the basin and unwrapped the bloodstained rags around Stephen's stump.

Esther sucked in her breath when he peeled off the last layer, and she could see where the leg had been cut off, right below the knee. It had started to scab over and looked terribly painful, but she watched determinedly as the doctor showed her how to dress the wound.

When he had finished cleaning and re-bandaging Stephen's stump, he wiped his hands on his dirty coat. "Do you still want to do this for your brother?" he asked quietly.

Esther took a deep breath. "Yes, I want to take him home. Will you please teach me what I need to know?"

The doctor shoved his spectacles farther up his nose and nodded. "Certainly."

"Esther, I'm going to go sit with David." Her father touched her shoulder and left.

"I'll come later," she promised, and as she followed the doctor to the next bed, Stephen flashed her an encouraging smile.

Esther could soon recognize what most wounds needed, but it never grew easier to see the men's pain. Some of them, like Stephen, had already lost an arm or a leg, and the doctor told her more would from infection.

The doctor introduced himself after they'd been working for nearly half an hour. "I'm Doctor Anderson," he said, handing her a bandage. "What is your name?"

"Esther Sullivan."

"Then, Esther Sullivan, you will do the next one by yourself."

So she did. She hesitated at first, but when the doctor didn't correct her, she went on with more confidence. When she finished, he motioned to the next bed.

"Keep working up this row."

Esther stared after him. *By myself?* She took her rags and basin of water to the skinny soldier in the next bed and gave him a smile. *Well, I'll have to take care of David by myself. Doctor Anderson is making me practice.*

When it was time to serve the men their supper, Esther helped distribute the food. Then she took two bowls of soup and a couple slices of bread to David's bed. Her father was sitting at its foot, and she handed him one of the bowls.

"Are you hungry, David?" she asked, sitting beside him.

He took the bowl from her. "Yes, but I can't move my arm."

"Here." Esther reached for the bowl. "I'll hold it for you."

David gave her a grateful smile. "Thank you, Little Birdie."

"Esther, you forgot to get a bowl for yourself," her father pointed out. "Would you like some of mine?"

She shook her head. "I can eat later." Hearing a noise, she turned to see Doctor Anderson at the foot of the bed with a basin in his hands. "I am going to change my water," he told her, "and bring it back so you can dress his wounds."

"All right." Esther swallowed hard. *I'll hate hurting David*, she thought. *It'll be worse than with strangers.*

The doctor strode away, and she watched David spoon in more soup.

"How are things at home?" he asked.

She glanced at him. It seemed like several years had passed since they left home. "Busy, of course," she said. "We are done with hay for this year, and the corn doesn't need hoed anymore, but you know how the work is never done."

"Has anyone ridden Triangle since I left?" David scraped the bottom of the bowl.

Esther tipped it so he could reach the rest of the soup. "I rode her a couple times this summer, and Peter's ridden her some too, but I think she misses you."

"Peter? You mean Peter Washburn?"

"Yes." Esther swiped a curl out of her face. "He still wants to join the army."

"He wouldn't if he knew what it was like. I'll have to tell him." David ate his last bite of bread. "That was good," he declared.

The doctor came back and helped Esther unstrap David's leg from the board. She unwrapped the bandage, trying not to think about how helpless her brother looked.

"Milksop is going to freshen this spring," she informed him. "What do you think we should name the baby?"

"That depends on what it is, of course," David pointed out. "But if it's a girl, I think we should name it Daisy."

Esther smiled at him. "Daisy would be perfect," she agreed.

"Why Daisy?" Carter wanted to know.

"Is he always this intrusive?" Esther asked her brother.

David laughed. "He's usually worse." Turning his head in Carter's direction, he explained, "Daisies were my mama's favorite flowers."

Carter looked half-scornful, half-disappointed. "So that wasn't your sweetheart's name, after all." Then he paused. "*Were* her favorite?"

David nodded. "She died last year. The same day that we lost the First Battle of Bull Run."

Carter was quiet after that. When Esther finished wrapping a clean bandage around David's leg, the doctor nodded and stepped back, adjusting his spectacles. "I have to go take care of the other patients," he said, turning to leave. "You are doing well with your brother."

Esther smiled after him, and David nudged her hand. "Esther, are you going to do my shoulder?"

"Of course." She unwound the bandage and carefully washed his shoulder before rewrapping it.

She spent the rest of the evening washing dirty dishes in a makeshift kitchen. When she wrapped herself in a quilt and rolled under the wagon to lie beside her father, she was exhausted.

11. Switching Armies

The next morning Esther watched as Doctor Anderson examined David's leg and shoulder.

"He slept better last night than he has for a while. And he looks happier." The doctor turned to her. "Are you sure you still want to take care of him?"

Esther nodded. "Yes, sir. I will do my best to make sure he gets better."

Doctor Anderson studied her, his pale blue eyes unreadable. "What happens if he dies after you get him home?"

Esther blinked at him. "If he dies?" she repeated slowly. "He will be at home in his own bed with his family. That's better than dying in a hospital."

The lines across the doctor's forehead relaxed. "All right, then. You can take him home."

Cheers erupted from all the men within hearing distance, and Carter hurrahed louder than anyone.

There certainly isn't much privacy in this place, Esther thought. But it didn't matter when she glanced around and saw the men's smiles.

"Have you ever considered becoming a nurse, Miss Sullivan?" Doctor Anderson asked.

Esther turned to meet his gaze. "A nurse?"

"Yes. You are a quick learner, and you don't seem queasy." He smiled. "You did an excellent job yesterday."

"Oh." Esther glanced at her father. "Well, I only want to be David's nurse right now."

The doctor shrugged. "Are you planning to leave right away?"

"As soon as we can get David into the wagon," Esther's father said.

Doctor Anderson helped strap David's leg to the board that came to his knee and fastened the makeshift sling he'd been using. In the bed beside them, Carter raised himself up on one elbow.

"Good-bye, Lieutenant Sullivan." He saluted. "I hope you get better soon."

David reached across to shake Carter's hand. "Same to you."

Carter nodded and sank back. "Thanks."

Esther's father and the doctor carried David out to the wagon, and Esther ran ahead to spread out some blankets for him.

"You'd better leave before I change my mind," the doctor said when David was settled.

Esther smiled at him. "Don't worry, Doctor Anderson. There is a doctor in our town, and I'll ask him to help me, I promise. Good-bye, and thank you for everything."

"You're welcome. Behave yourself, young man." He waved as they drove off.

As they left Centreville, Esther worried that David's leg wound might break open again, even though the horses were only walking. When they reached a creek and stopped for lunch, she asked him how the ride felt.

"It is rather bumpy," he admitted, "but it isn't as bad as I thought it would be. These blankets help." He fingered the quilt under him.

"Good." She smiled and went to help her father water the team.

David was asleep when she took the lunch basket from under the wagon seat. As she carried it around to the end of the wagon, he screamed and sat up.

"I am sorry!" he cried. Then his shoulders slumped. "Oh, God," he groaned. "He's dead."

Esther stepped back. He was staring right at her—or perhaps right through her. Realizing he was still asleep, she scrambled up beside him and shook his good shoulder.

"David! Wake up." He moaned, and she shook him again. "David. Everything is going to be all right. It was only a bad dream."

David shuddered and looked up at her. "Yes, it was a dream," he said huskily as his father came up. "But it was true."

"Do you want to tell us about it?" his father asked, studying David's pale face.

David sucked in a shaky breath. "It's the same awful nightmare every time. I keep remembering Matthew Westcott's eyes. The light…just flickered and went out." He stared into the distance.

"I killed lots of men, like Carter said," he continued, looking at his father. "And it was wrong. *I* was wrong." His voice rose a notch. "I'm sorry, Dad. I've never felt so guilty before. How can I ever make it right?"

Esther's father climbed into the wagon beside David. "You will never be able to make it right to the men you killed, son, but you can make it right with God."

"I want to," David said. "But how?"

Esther's father reached for his Bible and read from Psalms 51. "A broken and a contrite heart, O God, thou wilt not despise." He flipped to the third chapter of John in the New Testament. "For God sent not his Son into the world to condemn the world; but that the world through him might be saved.

"Jesus took all your guilt with him to the cross, David. If you repent and give him your life, God will forgive you and remember your sins no more."

Esther shifted as David stared at his father. At last he nodded and bowed his head.

"Dear God," he prayed quietly. "I think you know everything about me, and I want to say that I am sorry—so sorry for turning my back on you and doing what I wanted. Please forgive me and let me start again."

He paused, and Esther saw him smile. "From now on," David continued, "I will be a soldier in your army and take orders only from you. Thank you for taking my guilt. Amen."

David raised his head after a long moment, his eyes shining. "It feels like a weight has been lifted from my mind," he murmured. "I finally feel clean inside. And at peace. God is amazing!"

His father closed the Bible, and Esther saw tears in his eyes. "Yes, he is," he agreed.

They started north again and reached home the first week of October. Esther sighed in relief as their house and its familiar surroundings came into view.

"We're home, David!" she exclaimed.

As they drove in the lane, Triangle's whinny came from the Washburns' pasture.

David smiled. "That horse has an uncanny sense of knowing things."

"Dad, can David share your room until he's better?" Esther asked as her father stopped the team beside the porch steps. "It will be so much easier than taking him upstairs."

"He can have it all to himself." Her father's eyes twinkled. "Even with only one good leg, he'll probably kick too much for me."

Esther smiled and ran upstairs to the linen closet. When she had changed the sheets on her father's bed, she went out and found her father helping David up the porch steps.

"I hate to do this to you, David," she said, seeing her brother's pale face, "but you need a bath before you get into that clean bed. You are filthy."

He groaned. "Esther, please don't make me take a bath. How would I manage that with this splint?"

Esther bit her lip. "You're right. Doctor Anderson said to leave it on for at least three more weeks." She looked at him pleadingly. "Could you maybe wash up a bit, though? I'll unload the wagon and take it over to the Washburns. When I get back, I'll make supper, and we can eat and have devotions in Dad's room. All right?"

David nodded. "I guess I can wash up, if Dad will help me."

Esther squeezed his arm. "Thanks, David. I know you're tired."

Once the wagon was empty, Esther drove the team to the Washburns. She could see through the window that they were eating supper, and after knocking, she opened the door.

"We're back," she announced.

Mrs. Washburn stood up, placing her napkin on the table. "Did you find David, Esther?" she asked. "How is he?"

"He has a broken leg, and his shoulder's hurt, but he's getting better," Esther told them.

"Can we come over and see him?" Peter said eagerly.

"Not now!" Esther exclaimed.

"I didn't mean now," Peter said hastily. "Maybe tomorrow afternoon?"

"We wouldn't stay long," Mrs. Washburn assured her. "It would just be nice to say hello to David."

Esther nodded. "Certainly. I brought the team over," she said, glancing back to where the horses were waiting, "and I thought I could take Triangle and Milksop home. Thank you so much for taking care of them."

"You're welcome. I'm glad we could help you out." Mrs. Washburn turned to her son. "Peter, will you go take care of the team and help Esther get their animals?"

After leading Milksop and Triangle back home, Esther hurried inside. She found David lying on the living room sofa.

"He's falling asleep, Esther," her father said, pushing aside David's dirty blue coat and trousers. "I'm going to help him to bed."

By the time supper was ready, David was fast asleep, and Esther and her father ate alone.

12. Visitors

David ate an enormous portion at breakfast, and Esther had just begun to worry that there wouldn't be enough when he announced he was full. As she was heating water to dress David's wounds, she saw Doctor Cunningham's carriage drive in the lane. They had left a message with his wife on their way through Kirksville asking him to stop in and see David.

Esther carried a bowl of water to her parents' bedroom and put it on the floor. "Doctor Cunningham is here," she said.

As she spoke, the door opened. "In here," Esther heard her father say, and the two men came into the bedroom.

"How was life in the army?" Doctor Cunningham greeted David, shaking his hand. "Different than you expected?"

David nodded. "Yes. I am glad to be alive and back home again."

Doctor Cunningham sighed. "Too many of our men haven't made it home," he said. "Who has been taking care of you?"

David glanced down at the splint on his leg. "A doctor near Manassas Junction patched me up," he said. "Esther has been looking after me since they came down to get me."

"Is that right?" Doctor Cunningham swung to face her. When she nodded, he said, "Suppose you go ahead and dress his wounds, Miss Esther."

Esther did, and the doctor examined David's leg and shoulder closely. "I think your shoulder has mended, David," he said, "though it may always be stiff. Your leg seems to be healing well also.

"Miss Esther, you make a fine nurse. His shoulder shouldn't need a bandage anymore. I'll stop by again near the end of this week," he concluded.

Esther thanked him for his help, and he followed her father out of the room.

"It's nice to know that your shoulder is better." Esther sat down in the chair beside David's bed. "You should get some rest now, because the Washburns are coming over this afternoon."

She gave him a significant look, and David returned it.

The Washburns came an hour after lunch, and Esther stood beside her father as he held open the door. "Hello, and do come in," he welcomed them.

As they entered, Esther saw that their oldest girl was not with them.

"Where is Lydia?" she asked Mrs. Washburn.

Mrs. Washburn turned to her. "Haven't you heard?"

"No. Heard what?"

"Lydia is doing volunteer work in town," Mrs. Washburn explained, following the rest of her family into the bedroom.

Esther wanted to ask what kind of work, but Mrs. Washburn had gone forward to say hello to David.

Peter pushed through his siblings to David's bed. "What was it like, David?" He surveyed the bandaged leg like it was a badge of honor as he shook David's hand.

"It's not something I recommend." David's face was sober, but his tone was lighter than Esther expected. "I hear you've been riding Triangle for me," he continued.

"Oh, yes," Peter assented cheerfully. "She is fun to ride."

Esther took the children out to the barn, and they played hide-and-seek for nearly an hour. When they came back in, she uncovered the plate of cookies Mrs. Washburn had brought and said they could each have one.

"What kind of volunteer work is Lydia doing?" she asked Peter's twin sister Priscilla.

Priscilla's mouth was full of cookie, so Peter answered instead. "She is part of a group of women who make clothes, food, blankets, bandages, and other things to send to our men, and she's also helping out at the General Store, because Mr. Taylor's clerk left last month to enlist."

Esther fetched a cloth to wipe the cookie crumbs off Margaret's hands. "I wonder what your parents and Dad and David are talking about," she said.

Peter shrugged and grabbed a cookie. "Let's go see," he suggested.

As soon as Margaret saw her mother, she began to fuss, and Mr. and Mrs. Washburn said it was time for them to go home.

After seeing them out the door, Esther went back into the bedroom and sat down at the foot of David's bed. "How are you feeling by now?" she asked with a weary grin.

He looked tired too, but his smile was cheerful. "I'm all right. Thanks for taking the children out to the barn and keeping them entertained."

Esther laughed. "They entertained themselves. What did you talk about in here?"

David shrugged. "Among other things, we talked about Peter and how he wants to join the army."

Esther sat up straighter. "They're not going to let him, are they?"

David shook his head. "No. They don't want him to get hurt. I need to talk to Peter, though. He might run off to join without his parents' permission."

"Maybe they should just let him go like Dad did with you, and he can find out for himself what really happens during a war."

"No plan works the same for everyone." Esther's father rubbed the back of his neck.

Several days after they had gotten home, Esther was in the garden digging potatoes. When her bucket was almost full, she stopped, leaning one arm on her potato fork to rest. A breeze fanned her hot face, and she wiped her forehead on her sleeve.

Out in the pasture, Triangle whinnied. Esther was surprised to hear a horse behind her answer Triangle with a nicker. She turned, expecting to see the Washburns or Doctor Cunningham. But there on the lane stood Daniel Armstrong, holding the reins of his black horse.

I wonder when he arrived, she thought, tucking a stray curl behind her ear.

He left Raven and came toward her, pulling off his cap. "Hello, Esther."

Esther stuck her fork into the ground and dropped a quick curtsy. "Hello," she said, returning his smile. "What brings you here?"

"I came to see David." Daniel glanced at the house. "I visited him at the hospital in Centreville and told him I would come again, so he wrote to let me know that he wasn't there anymore."

"Come on inside. He'll be happy to see you." Esther wiped her hands on her apron and picked up the bucket of potatoes.

"Here." Daniel stepped closer. "I'll carry that for you."

"Thank you." Esther handed it to him, and they started toward the house. "Are you going to leave Raven on the lane?" she asked.

"Don't worry. He won't run off."

Esther glanced at the horse again. "Do you mind if I unsaddle him and put him in the barn after I take you to David? He'll get hot standing in the sun."

Daniel looked at her for a moment. "It wouldn't be the first time he was left in the sun, but if you want to, go ahead."

When they were inside, he set the bucket down and followed her into the bedroom.

"Look who came, David," she announced.

Her brother looked up from reading the Bible. "Daniel!" he exclaimed. "I wasn't expecting to see you."

"After reading your letter, I wanted to talk to you." Daniel shook David's outstretched hand. "How are you doing?"

David shrugged and nodded. "All right."

Esther slipped out and closed the door. *Now for Raven,* she thought with a smile, jumping off the porch steps. After tying him in Triangle's empty stall, she unsaddled him, brushed him down, and gave him hay.

Back in the kitchen, she made extra chicken dumplings for lunch. Hearing footsteps, she turned to see Daniel.

"David sent me to ask if you know where your father is," he said, leaning against the doorway.

Esther nodded. "He's over at the Washburns, our neighbors who live half a mile down the road. He will be back any minute. Will you stay to lunch?"

Daniel shrugged. "Only if you have enough. I don't want to impose."

"We have plenty," Esther told him. "You won't be imposing."

"Then I will. And thank you."

"Daniel!" David's voice came from the bedroom. "Did you get lost?"

Esther raised her eyebrows and smiled. "I wonder what he wants now."

"He's probably tired of talking to himself and needs someone else to talk to." Daniel chuckled and left.

Esther's father was coming up the porch steps when she went out to dump her dishwater. "Daniel Armstrong is here to see David," she told him.

"He is?" Her father went into the bedroom, and when Esther returned to the dining room, her brother was sitting in his chair, his leg sticking out to one side in its splint.

"David, it's so good to see you at the table!" she told him, setting out the dishes.

David laughed. "It's good to *be* at the table."

Later Daniel passed the dumplings to David and said, "I feel very sure the war will be over by Christmastime. The Southern army is not nearly as strong or well equipped as ours is. Surely they can't hold out much longer."

"That is what everyone said last year," Esther's father pointed out.

Daniel grinned. "That's true," he admitted. "I guess we will have to wait and see what happens."

"Who is your first lieutenant now?" David asked.

"Jack Mason stepped up to fill your place." Daniel's eyes twinkled. "He's helping me get the men back in shape."

David laughed. "Best wishes with that."

13. A Dying Soldier

Nearly a week after Daniel's visit, Esther was changing the bandage on her brother's leg and remembered his nightmare on their way home.

"What was it about Matthew Westcott that shook you up so badly?" she asked him. "Didn't you see other men die?"

David nodded. "I'll tell you about it," he said, and then was silent for a moment. "I was separated from my company during a retreat, and I tripped over a wounded Rebel. I jumped to my feet and was about to hurry on, but he opened his eyes and stared straight into my heart.

David's mouth twisted. "At least, that's how it felt to me. He begged me for a drink, so I gave him some water from my canteen. His legs had been blasted off, and there was a bullet hole in his chest, but he grabbed my arm with a strong grip and whispered, 'Stay a minute, young fellow. I need to tell you something.'

"I asked what, and he said, 'I forgive you for killing my countrymen.' He sighed. 'And yours.'"

David wiped his forehead and swallowed hard. "I blurted the first thing that came to my mind. 'Forgive me? But I never said I was sorry.'

"He said, 'I still forgive you. You are only following orders, same as me. But I've never been able to forget that each Yankee I shot had a family praying for his safe return. It's too late for me to do anything different, but it's not too late for you. I beg you to stop killing and go back home.'"

David paused. "I hadn't thought much about the Confederates I killed in the other battles, but Matthew Westcott's words changed that. I shot at Rebel soldiers twice more before I was wounded later that day, and each time I felt ashamed. Only on our way home when I asked God to forgive me did I stop feeling guilty."

Esther had finished re-bandaging David's leg and was sitting on the chair beside his bed. She leaned forward when he stopped. "But how did you know his name? Did he tell you?"

David shook his head. "He had a piece of paper pinned to his uniform with his name and address written on it. A lot of soldiers do that right before a battle."

He rubbed his face. "I will never forget the look in Matthew Westcott's eyes when he died," he finished huskily. "But God used his words to change me, and I'm grateful for that."

Esther squeezed his hand. "Thank you for telling me about it," she said.

He smiled. "Thank *you*, Little Birdie, for going all the way to Virginia to bring me home."

Doctor Cunningham had stopped in once a week since they brought David home, and in the middle of November he said, "You'll soon be out of bed for good, David."

"At last!" Esther exclaimed. She waltzed over and hugged her father. "I am so happy."

"I noticed," David said dryly.

She sat down on the chair beside his bed. "Aren't you?"

"Of course I am." He glanced down at his leg and then looked back up at her with a grin. "My joy just decided to stay inside of me instead of gushing out like yours is. But you have good reason to be excited." He gave her a special smile. "It's about time all your hard work paid off."

Esther sat back in her chair and returned his smile.

After a few more weeks, Doctor Cunningham gave David permission to start hobbling around. Esther helped him move his things upstairs, and he slept in his own bed again.

One evening after supper she took some clean clothes up to her room. Before she went back down, she stepped into her brother's room. "Is there anything I can do for you, David?"

He looked up at her. "Will you get the Bible from my chest of drawers and read me the sixty-second Psalm?"

Esther thought of the supper dishes that still needed to be washed and the cream that was waiting to be churned.

"Please, Little Birdie?"

"Sure." Esther grabbed the Bible, sat down in the chair, and flipped through the worn pages. "Which Psalm was it?"

"Sixty-two."

She found the place and started reading. The last two verses caught her attention. "God hath spoken once; twice have I heard this; that power belongeth unto God. Also unto thee, O Lord, belongeth mercy: for thou renderest unto every man according to his work.

"What does that mean, David?" she asked when she finished.

Her brother raised his eyebrows. "What does what mean?"

"The last thing I read. How can God be merciful and still give people what they deserve?"

David sat up and leaned against the wall. "I think to some extent God will judge people by whether they have done good or bad in this life, but that is not how he makes his final decision."

"How, then?"

He took the Bible from her. "God is holy and cannot be around sin. Any sin. Since he loves us, he sent his Son to take our sin and die in our place so we can be holy and have a relationship with him."

He turned to the third chapter of John in the New Testament. "He that believeth on the Son hath everlasting life; and he that believeth not the Son shall not see life; but the wrath of God abideth on him."

David closed the Bible. "God makes his final decision based on whether or not you have accepted the gift of his Son's sacrifice and asked him to make you holy."

"Oh." Esther nodded.

"Say"—David ran a hand through his hair—"can you cut my hair soon? It's getting a little hard to manage."

Esther reached out to touch it. It *was* getting pretty long.

He swatted her hand away. "I want you to cut it, not play with it."

"All right, all right." She stood up and started toward the door. "But not tonight. Maybe tomorrow."

He nodded. "Good night, Little Birdie."

"Good night, David."

Esther went over to her room and pulled her rocking chair to the window. She curled up in it, resting her chin on her knees as she looked outside. The few remaining patches of white from the last snowfall had melted during the day, and the sun was setting behind the trees at the far end of the field.

She stared at the streaks of pink and purple in the sky as she thought about what David had said. Ever since he had decided to resign from the Union Army and enlist in God's army, he'd had a new passion for life. Listening to him talk, she had almost felt left out, as if she was on the outside looking in at something good.

The pretty colors faded from the sky, leaving it a dull gray. Esther sighed and went downstairs to wash the supper dishes and churn the cream, feeling a sadness she could not explain.

14. Thank You, Little Birdie

It was light when Esther awoke two days later. She put a hand out from under her quilt and smiled when the air was warm. *Dad must have stoked the fires already,* she thought with a surge of gratefulness. *That makes it so much easier to get up.*

As she combed her hair, she remembered David's request for a haircut. *I'll do it today,* she planned. *Right after breakfast.*

She heard him call her name and went over to his room, greeting him with a cheerful, "Good morning."

He moved his good leg back and forth, knocking his quilt to the floor. "Esther, my leg hurts."

Esther dropped to her knees beside his bed and pulled up his trousers' leg. A swollen vein stretched down his calf from where the shell had broken his leg.

She looked up at him, her stomach twisting with fear. "I don't know what is wrong with it, David."

"There's a sharp pain in my chest when I breathe," he said slowly. "Will you go get Dad?" He coughed into his handkerchief, and she saw blood on the white cloth.

Esther dropped her comb and rushed out to the barn. "Dad," she hollered. "Daddy!" She found him milking Milksop.

"What is it?" The pail tipped as he stood up, spilling the milk into the straw.

Esther stumbled as she reached him and grabbed his arm to catch herself. "Daddy, something is wrong with David's leg," she gasped. "He's coughing up blood, and he said he can't breathe right."

"Oh, God, what now?" her father murmured, closing his eyes for a second.

Esther shook his arm. "He wants you, Daddy."

Her father grabbed her hand, and they ran to the house. When they reached David's room, Esther knelt beside the bed.

"Look at this, Dad."

There was a dark bulge below where David's bone had punctured his leg. The skin was stretched tight, like a puffy bee sting.

"What's wrong with it?" her father asked.

Esther shook her head. "I don't know!" She moved to sit on the chair. "Does it still hurt to breathe?"

David nodded. "It's getting worse." He coughed more blood into his handkerchief and glanced at his father. "Will you give Esther the letter I wrote?"

Esther saw tears in her father's eyes. He squeezed David's shoulder. "Of course."

"Thank you, Dad, for showing me the best way to live." David took a shuddery breath, wincing. "I couldn't have asked for a better father."

David's breathing grew more labored, and Esther stood up. He looked at her. "Esther, never think this was your fault." He reached for her hand and squeezed it. "You were a great nurse. Thank you, Little Birdie."

Esther shook her head frantically, her heart racing. "No! Stop acting like this, David. Dad, we must get Doctor Cunningham!"

Her father glanced at her as he crouched beside the bed and smoothed back David's damp, black hair with a calloused hand.

David struggled for breath, and his eyes flickered closed. The tense muscles in his jaw and forehead relaxed until his face was smooth and peaceful.

"David, no." Her father bowed his head on the bed, his voice trembling. "Dear God, not again."

Esther stared at her brother as the hand in hers went limp. She shook it. "No! He can't be dead. David!" She looked at her father. "Tell me he's not gone," she whispered.

Outside, Triangle whinnied.

Her father swallowed hard and sat back on his heels, still looking at his son. "He *is* gone, Esther. Even his horse knows." His voice broke.

"But I hadn't cut his hair yet!" she protested.

"Cut his hair?" her father repeated. He glanced over at her, and she saw tears on his cheeks.

"He was supposed to be getting better!" she cried, flinging David's cold hand away from her. She watched it land on the bed beside him. "If God is so good and kind and loving, why did he let this happen? And Mama? And this awful war?" Her voice rose. "Why, Dad?"

Slumping to the floor, she pulled her knees up to her chin and wrapped her arms around them.

After several minutes, her father came over and kissed the top of her head. She heard him take a shaky breath. "I am not God, to have those answers for you, Esther."

Esther let her head drop onto her knees, and her hair fell across her eyes. He said something else as he left the room, but all she heard was the last word.

Breakfast! Thinking about food made her feel sick. She looked at David, but her father had drawn the sheet over his face. All she could see was his right leg, which always kicked off the quilt.

She hugged her knees and gulped, remembering the blanket-covered forms in Centreville's hospital. Doctor Anderson's words came to haunt her. "What if he dies after you get him home?"

"Oh, why did he have to be right?" she burst out miserably. Her throat ached, but she couldn't cry.

Her comb was still on the floor, and she picked it up as she went out. But when she reached her room, she didn't feel like braiding her hair. *I'll go make some breakfast for Dad,* she decided and saw the unfinished plaque of Triangle on her chest of drawers.

"I know it looks a little strange now, but I'll finish it as soon as I can. Maybe when I come home on leave, or when the war is over and I come home for good."

David's cheerful words flashed through her mind, and she slapped the plaque facedown into her top drawer. It landed beside all his letters, his discharge paper, *Highland Rose,* and her mother's necklace. Most of her letters to him were there too, because he had saved them.

"I didn't throw them away, but you can if you don't want them," he had said.

She'd exclaimed, "How sweet of you!" and hugged his good shoulder.

Memories of him threatened to overwhelm her. She shoved the drawer closed and left the room.

15. Grieving

When her father came in, he looked surprised to see her setting food on the table. "I said I could fix us something to eat if you didn't feel like making breakfast."

Esther paused. "Is that what you said? I only heard the last word."

They sat down, and her father prayed. Esther glanced at David's chair, her mind shutting out his words.

David was just starting to sit in it again, she thought. *How can I stand seeing it empty from now on?*

"Esther?"

Her father's voice jerked her out of her thoughts. She could see by his expression that he was worried about her, but she didn't say anything. After a bit, he picked up his spoon, staring at it for a long moment before he took his first bite.

"I'm actually not that hungry, but since you've already made it…" He slowly continued eating his oatmeal.

Out of habit, Esther served herself some. She usually liked oatmeal, but this morning it looked unappetizing and tasted slimy.

"After we are finished eating," her father said, "I will ask Mr. Washburn and Peter to dig a grave for David before this thaw ends."

Esther coughed, choking on her oatmeal. It slid past the lump in her throat, and she forced herself to continue eating.

"Thank you for making breakfast." Her father's voice broke into her thoughts again. "But I don't mind skipping lunch." He touched her arm. "So don't make anything unless you want to."

Esther bit her lip, staring at her bowl. "I think it's better if I have something to do."

He nodded and put on his coat and hat. Stopping at the door, he came back to the table, and Esther felt him watching her.

She dropped her spoon into her bowl and looked up at him. "Go on. I will be fine here by myself."

"All right then," he said at last. "If you're sure."

She suddenly wasn't so sure anymore. But she didn't say anything, and he left, squeezing her shoulder gently. Although she felt like curling up in her chair, she put the food away. She'd forgotten that David wouldn't be asking for seconds of oatmeal, so she had cooked way too much.

When she washed the two bowls and spoons from breakfast, she wondered how long it would be before she was only washing her own dishes. She felt like screaming as she flung the dishwater violently across the yard.

Esther shifted on the sofa, tucking her skirt around her feet. She heard a knock on the door but didn't move.

The door opened and closed, and Lydia Washburn appeared in the living room doorway. "Hello, Esther," she said softly.

Esther gazed at her. "Hello," she said finally.

Lydia came and knelt beside her. "I am so sorry about David. Is there anything I can do for you?"

Esther shrugged.

"Would you like me to comb your hair?" Lydia asked.

"If you want to. My comb is in my room."

Esther led the way upstairs and knelt silently in front of her chest of drawers while Lydia braided her hair and twisted it into a bun.

"Thank you, Lydia. It looks nice." She turned from the looking glass. "Did you come over alone?"

"No. I came with Father and Peter." Lydia laid down the comb. "Mother sent you some bread. I left it on the table."

They went downstairs to the dining room, and Lydia motioned to a covered plate on the table. "I baked it yesterday."

Esther felt a lump in her throat. "Thank you."

Lydia nodded. "I'll see you this afternoon, but I should probably run on home now."

"What is this afternoon?" Esther fingered the braids against the side of her head.

"David's funeral. Your father said he wanted to have it right away," Lydia explained. "Since it's so soon I doubt as many people will come as when your mama died."

"I won't mind that," Esther said. "The last thing I want right now is a lot of people telling me how sorry they are for me and how they know exactly how I feel."

Lydia looked stricken.

"Oh, I didn't mean you," Esther added hastily. "I am glad you came over." She hugged Lydia. "I feel a little better now. Thank you."

Lydia hugged her back. "You're welcome. Good-bye." She threw her shawl around her shoulders and went out with a little wave.

Esther carried the bread to the kitchen table. Not knowing what else to do, she found her shawl, wrapped it around her shoulders, and went out to stand on the porch. She could see Lydia entering the woods on the little path where a bridge crossed the stream. Glancing across the field, she saw Mr. Washburn and Peter digging a hole beside her mother's grave.

She stumbled down the steps and walked to the barn, her ears ringing with the steady blows of a hammer. As she slipped inside, the noise ceased. She picked up a currycomb and went to Triangle's stall, nudging the horse over.

Looking past the mare, Esther saw her father bent over a half-finished box. She froze, seeing his shoulders start to shake. He gripped the wood, and a sob broke the silence.

Triangle nickered, and Esther stole toward her father.

"Daddy," she whispered, tugging his hand away from the coffin. She wrapped her arms around his neck, and he pulled her close, still crying.

They stood there for a long moment, Esther feeling an unbearable sadness as she clung to him.

"Thank you, sweetheart." He sniffed, releasing her and wiping his eyes.

"Do you think Mr. Washburn and Peter will stay to lunch?" she asked him.

He shook his head and picked up his hammer again. "Mr. Washburn and Peter are not *allowed* to stay to lunch. Mrs. Washburn told them they had to go back home."

"Oh." Esther watched him pound in two more pegs. "Then I'll go make lunch for us."

As she finished washing the lunch dishes, Doctor Cunningham's black carriage rattled into their lane. Her father met him at the door, and she heard them go upstairs.

She went outside again, and since Mr. Washburn and Peter had gone home, she walked out and stared down into the hole they had dug. Loneliness swept over her, and she returned to the house, collapsing onto the living room sofa.

"Esther, wake up."

Esther opened her eyes to see her father. She could hear a jumble of voices somewhere outside.

"It's time for the funeral, Esther," her father said, squeezing her hand. "The minister just arrived."

She sat up and rubbed her face. "My dress is all wrinkled. May I go change?"

"Of course." He stepped back as she stood up. "We'll wait."

It only took her a minute to change into a clean dress. When she went back downstairs, her father hugged her.

"I love you, Esther," he whispered. "We'll get through this together."

Outside, he, Mr. Washburn, Peter, and Mr. Taylor, the owner of the General Store in town, picked up David's coffin and started walking across the field.

Esther walked behind them, in front of the rest of the Washburns, Doctor Cunningham, and their other friends. She stumbled through the muddy rows of corn stubble and stopped when the men set the coffin down at the edge of the hole.

The minister began talking as she stared at the coffin, pegged shut. When the men stepped forward to lower it into the hole, she suddenly felt desperate to see her brother again. This was her last chance before he was forever buried in the ground.

"Wait!" she cried, lunging forward and grabbing the side of the coffin. "Open it up," she pleaded. "I want to see him one more time."

She felt her father's hands on her shoulders. "Esther?" he said softly. "Come away."

She shook her head, still clinging to the coffin. "I have to see him. Please."

"All right, then." He picked up a shovel and used the tip to pry up two boards.

Esther bent over the opening. She knew her brother's face as well as her own, but as she stared at the lifeless face in the coffin, despair filled her.

She backed away. Her father replaced the pegs, and the men lowered the coffin into the ground.

David's dead. He's dead!

Esther wanted to scream. She clamped a hand over her mouth, forcing herself to stay where she was until the dirt was mounded over her brother's coffin.

Then she fled to the house, followed by a dull thudding sound as her father pounded in a wooden cross. She ran up the stairs to her room and slammed the door. Grabbing her pillow from her bed, she sank to the floor in the farthest corner.

"No!" she screamed, pressing her face into the pillow. "Please, David! Don't leave me." *How can I go on living?* she thought frantically.

"David, you were nearly well," she moaned. "Why did this happen? No! Please, no!"

After a long time, the door opened and closed, and she heard someone walking around downstairs. Then the fourth step creaked, and by the time the footsteps reached the landing, she recognized her father's heavy tread.

He rapped on her door. "Esther?" he called softly. "Are you in there? Are you all right?"

She was silent.

After a moment he continued. "I will be downstairs if you need me. Don't worry about making supper. I'll find something to eat." He paused. "I love you, Esther."

She stared at the door as his footsteps descended the stairs, suddenly wishing she'd answered him. "Daddy," she whispered, aching to be clasped in his strong, comforting arms.

Leaning her head against the wall, she pulled her knees up and pounded her pillow with her fists. She must have fallen asleep, because sometime during the night she awoke, stiff and miserable.

"David is gone," she whimpered, gripping her pillow. Her room was cold, and she shivered as she crept into bed.

16. Riding and Running

After breakfast the next morning, which she forced herself to make and eat for her father's sake, Esther took her shawl and wandered out to the barn. Triangle looked out from her stall and nickered. Esther went over and started petting the mare's brown neck. The smooth muscles under her hand gave her an idea.

Slipping the bridle over Triangle's ears and fastening it, she led the mare out to the pasture. She halted Triangle beside the fence and climbed high enough to slide onto the mare's back. Urging the horse forward, she held the reins in one hand and felt her muscles relax as she sat back into the rhythm of the horse's strides.

Triangle walked around the pasture, and as they passed under a tree outside the fence, a small, dead branch fell on her hind-quarters. She bounded sideways, and Esther grabbed a handful of her mane to keep from falling.

The mare slowed, but when Esther dug in her heels to regain her balance, she took off again. Still holding the reins, Esther leaned forward and locked her hands under Triangle's neck as the mare galloped along the pasture fence. Triangle's mane whipped into Esther's face and brought tears to her eyes.

Triangle galloped all the way around the pasture before slowing. Tears from the stinging wind streamed down Esther's face, and somehow a little of the pain inside her trickled away with them. She sucked in a deep breath and sat up, wiping her cheeks.

Triangle had stopped near the barn. Esther glanced around and saw her father sitting on the fence.

"Esther, are you all right?"

She stared at his anxious face and nodded, nudging Triangle closer.

"I only wanted her to walk, but when she spooked and galloped around the pasture, the wind made me cry, and now I feel better. I haven't been able to cry since—" She stopped.

"I saw you almost fall off." He jumped down from the fence and held Triangle's bridle while she slid off. He turned her to face him. "It scared me, Esther. Please be careful."

"I will, Dad." She took Triangle's reins. "I should walk her around so she can cool down."

He nodded and let her go.

It snowed, Esther realized the next morning, looking out the kitchen window. The trees were outlined in white and glistened in the sun.

"Please don't ride Triangle in this snow, Esther," her father said during breakfast.

Esther jerked her head up. "I wasn't going to."

He nodded. "Doctor Cunningham said that the bulge in David's leg was a blood clot. He said no one could have prevented it."

Esther swallowed her last bite and took her dishes to the kitchen.

I wish it was nice enough to ride, she thought later, after lunch. *I must do* something.

Taking her shawl from its peg by the door, she went outside. Hurrying out the lane, she shivered and walked down the road away from town. Before long, she tied the ends of her shawl together and ran to keep warm. The cold air rushing past her face drove everything from her mind, and she ran until she collapsed in a snow bank beside the road.

She felt warm, but she could hardly move her toes. Her breathing gradually returned to normal, and she stood up. Hearing the crunch of footsteps, she turned to see her father running toward her.

"Esther, why are you out in this cold?" he panted.

Esther pulled her shawl tighter. "I'm only trying to keep my mind off—" She gritted her chattering teeth and plunged on. "Off David. You don't have to follow me around. I'll be all right, Dad. I have to be."

Her father wrapped his coat and his arms around her, and she clung to him. "Yes, you will be," he murmured, his cheek against her hair. "I'm praying for you, sweetheart."

They walked back to the house together and sat in front of the fire.

Esther went for a walk nearly every day after that. She couldn't bear being cooped up in the house, and after being outside, she always felt refreshed.

One day near the end of February, she had walked over a mile up the road. As she stepped off a bridge, she slipped. The creek bank was sloped, and she shrieked as she tumbled down into the shallow, icy water.

Climbing the bank, she shivered, trying to wring out her skirts. As she stumbled up the road, her teeth chattered, and her breath sent out little white clouds.

"Just...get...home," she told herself. Her clothes stiffened in the cold air, and she could barely feel her fingers and toes.

When she finally reached the porch and tried to open the door, her hands were too numb to turn the knob. She heard footsteps, and her father opened the door, gasping when he saw her.

"Dad?" She swayed, and he caught her arm.

"Esther? What happened to you?"

"So cold," she mumbled, her teeth chattering.

He pulled her inside and hurried her into the living room. She stood in front of the fire, her clothes dripping onto the floor. Her father brought a towel and her nightgown and waited in the dining room until she'd changed.

Esther's fingers started stinging, and she shook them. "Daddy, it hurts."

"You're warming up too fast." He led her to the sofa. "Stay here, and I will fetch a blanket."

She flopped onto the sofa, and before long he came back to sit beside her.

"Will you tell me what happened?"

She shivered and clutched the blanket he tucked around her. "I was just walking. But I slipped and fell into a creek. It took me so long to reach home."

He shook his head. "Esther, please stop taking walks in this cold weather."

She looked up and saw the seriousness in his eyes. "All right, I'll stop."

"Thank you." He sighed. "You are all I have left, and I can't lose you too."

She snuggled closer to him and whispered, "I love you, Daddy."

He put his arms around her and pressed his cheek against her damp hair. "I love you too."

Only then, warmed by the fire and his love, could she stop trembling.

The war dragged on. Mr. Washburn brought them news of a battle near Fredericksburg, Virginia, at the beginning of December and then another one at Stones River in January.

On March third, the North passed a draft law. It was the same day that Milksop had her calf, and Esther named the velvety heifer Daisy.

Spring came, and Esther's father spent his days in the field with Triangle, plowing. One evening in mid-April, Esther went outside and found her father sitting on the porch steps. He was gazing across the field to where the sun was slipping behind a bank of orange-tinted clouds. She sat on the lowest step and cupped her chin in one hand, watching the brilliant colors fade.

"Have you heard about the draft law?"

She turned to look at him. "Yes. Peter told me."

"Peter?" He gave her a half-grin. "Yesterday I heard from Mr. Washburn that the fellows who are conscripting all the remaining able-bodied men are in this area."

"They are!" Her eyes widened. "What are you going to do if they come here? Will you hide?"

"It's a matter of *when* they come, not *if.*" He sighed. "I don't know what I'll do."

Icy prickles ran up her spine. "Please hide in the barn or in the root cellar or *somewhere*," she begged. "I don't want them to take you."

"Neither do I, and if God doesn't want them to find me, he will hide me better than any barn or root cellar can."

She searched his face and knew he wouldn't hide. "But what will I do if you are taken?"

"Stay here and take care of the farm." He took a deep breath. "If you can't do it on your own, I am sure the Washburns will help you. They'll probably even let you live with them, if you want."

"What if Mr. Washburn gets taken also?"

"You could still live with them. You would be as much of a help to them as they would be to you." He squeezed her shoulder. "I'm praying I won't be taken. We've finally started to get over losing David, but we still need each other."

She stared at him. "How do you mean?"

He shrugged. "I know I have to look out for you, and it helps me focus on something besides how much I miss him. I understand how you're hurting, Esther, because I am too. But it might help us to talk about him instead of pushing the hurt away."

Esther shook her head, feeling her stomach tighten. "No. Please, I can't." She wiped her clammy hands on her skirt and closed her eyes.

"Do you ever cry?" Her father's voice was quiet. "It's helped me."

She looked up at him. "No," she whispered. "I haven't been able to." She swallowed hard. "And I don't want to talk about him yet, but I'll come to you when I do."

He took her hand and pulled her up to sit beside him. "I'll wait, then," he said, putting his arm around her.

She laid her head on his shoulder and let out a long, shaky breath. "Dad," she whispered, "I still don't understand why God lets bad things happen."

After a moment of silence, he said softly, "God isn't asking you to. When you were little, did you understand everything Mama did?"

Esther shook her head. "No, and I was always asking her questions."

"Yes, but you didn't get upset because you didn't understand. You still loved her and wanted to be with her. It's the same way with God. The Bible says that his thoughts are not our thoughts, and his ways are not our ways. Don't bring him down to your level. Let him be God."

He paused. "And, Esther, he is big enough to make something good come from what we think is bad, like Mama and David dying. I'm always reminded of that whenever I see dark storm clouds edged in gold."

Esther stared out into the twilight, watching the blinking fireflies. The stillness calmed her, and when they stood to go inside, she whispered, "I'm glad you're my dad."

He smiled at her. "I'm glad you're my daughter."

17. Psalm Fifty-Seven: One

Esther smiled as she made sandwiches for her father's lunch the next day. *Only a few more days until the plowing is finished,* she thought. *Then we have to do the planting.* As she put the sandwiches in a basket and draped a cloth over the top, a movement outside the window caught her eye.

A group of men stood near the road, and two of them started toward the porch. One was carrying a rifle, and the other had a pistol in his belt. It wasn't until she opened the door in response to the men's knocking that she realized who they were.

The recruiters Dad told me about!

Her heart beat faster. *What am I supposed to do?* Glancing toward the field, she realized her father was in the section hidden by a strip of woods. She took a deep breath.

"Good morning, gentlemen. What can I do for you?"

The shorter of the two men, the one with the rifle, touched his cap. "Good morning, miss," he said pleasantly. "I need to speak with your father."

"My father?" Esther tried to look apologetic. "He isn't here right now."

The taller man squinted at her. The spokesman frowned and asked, "Do you know when he will be back?"

Esther opened her mouth to say he would return that evening and saw Triangle step from behind the trees. Her heart sank, and she forgot what she was going to say.

The taller man followed her gaze. "Shipley, look," he said, pointing.

Shipley threw a glance over his shoulder at Esther as he and his companion left the porch. She kicked the door as they started across the field toward her father. He saw them coming and pulled Triangle to a halt.

Esther slumped against the doorframe. *God, they're going to take my dad!* she wailed silently. *Please don't let this happen!*

The men were talking to her father, and then Triangle was walking again. Her father left the plow at the edge of the field and took Triangle to the barn. The men followed him inside, reappearing after several minutes.

The taller man led Triangle, un-harnessed now, to the group of men, and Shipley accompanied her father to the house. "We will give you some time to say good-bye to your family," he said as they reached the porch. "You may collect a few personal items to bring along, but you won't need to pack clothes, since the army will issue you a uniform."

Esther's father nodded, leading her inside. "I'll be out in a few minutes," he told Shipley quietly, closing the door.

"He sounded like he was reciting a speech!" Esther burst out.

Her father sighed. "Yes, I imagine he's said those words quite a few times the past several days. Now, Esther, we only have a few minutes, so I am going to get some things from—"

"Why are they taking Triangle?" she interrupted him.

"The army always needs good horses," he reminded her, starting for his bedroom. "Just like it always needs good men."

Esther caught her breath. *The army won't think Dad is a good man when he refuses to fight!* She followed him into the bedroom. "Dad?"

"Yes?" He looked up from the things he was wrapping in a blanket.

"Oh, Dad." She bit her lip. "What will happen when they find out you won't fight?"

For a moment his eyes were worried. Then he said lightly, "I don't know. Maybe they will send me home. You think?"

"I wish they would." She knew he was brushing her off and didn't say any more.

"Esther, I want you to read Psalms fifty-seven verse one, and do what it says. Can you remember that? Psalms fifty-seven: one?"

Raising her eyes to meet his, she nodded numbly.

"Come here, sweetheart." He hugged her as he went on talking. "You can stay here or go to the Washburns like we talked about last night. I will pray for you every day, and God will take care of you."

"I think I will stay here," she decided hesitantly, "and look after Milksop and Daisy."

"That's fine," he approved. "I will write to you as soon as I can."

Esther closed her eyes, listening to the confidence in his voice. *What will I do without you, Daddy?*

"I love you," he whispered, releasing her. He picked up his bundle and walked out of the house.

She went into the kitchen to look out the window and saw the basket of sandwiches on the table. Snatching it up, she dashed outside. "Dad, wait!"

She caught up with him as he and Shipley reached the group of men. "Here." She held out the basket. "Your lunch."

"Thank you, Esther." He kissed her forehead as Shipley motioned him and the others to start walking. "I'll be praying for you," he called over his shoulder.

She fixed her eyes on his dark hair as he headed up the road, surrounded by the other men. When they reached the bend in the road and she lost sight of him, she felt desperately alone.

"Daddy!" she screamed. Her cry echoed in the silence. *David and Dad both disappeared around that bend because of the war,* she thought, her heart sinking. *David died. Oh, God, what will happen to Dad?*

Going back to the house, she took the Bible to the dining room table. Finding the place, she ran her finger under the words as she read the verse aloud.

"Be merciful unto me, O God, be merciful unto me: for my soul trusteth in thee: yea, in the shadow of thy wings will I make my refuge, until these calamities be overpast."

She bit her lip, catching sight of the words in the next column. "What time I am afraid, I will trust in thee. In God have I put my trust: I will not be afraid what man can do unto me."

Closing the Bible, she sank into a chair. *All right, Daddy, I understand.*

"I suppose I should go tell the Washburns," she said at last. Returning the Bible to the mantel, she struck out across the field and through the woods to the Washburns' house.

When Peter finally answered Esther's knock, his face was more sober than she had ever seen it.

"Hello, Peter," she said, after he had stared silently at her for several seconds. "What's wrong?"

"I can't tell you," he said in a miserable voice, turning away. "Come ask Mother."

Esther stepped inside and closed the door, frowning. Margaret was wailing in her cradle, Priscilla was arguing with Sarah, her next youngest sister, and Victoria huddled silently in a corner. The three younger boys were shoving each other around. Mrs. Washburn sat at the table with her head in her hands, crying, and Lydia was rubbing her mother's shoulders.

Those recruiters must have taken Mr. Washburn too, Esther thought. *But I didn't see him with the group of men, and since they were headed toward town, they must have stopped here already.*

"What is it, Lydia? What happened?"

"Oh, Esther!" Tears rolled down Lydia's cheeks. "My father took a barrel of lard to Uncle Thomas' this morning. A while ago Uncle Thomas came rushing up on a horse. He said that my father's wagon had collided with another wagon in a horrible accident, and he thinks Father is dead."

"Dead!" Esther's eyes widened. "Lydia, I am so sorry." She put her arm around Lydia.

The door burst open behind them, and Mr. Washburn limped in. Esther shook Mrs. Washburn's shoulder. "Look," she said. "He's not dead."

For a moment there was silence, aside from Margaret's wailing. Then Mrs. Washburn started crying again, Lydia's mouth dropped open, Peter brightened, and Priscilla and Sarah smiled.

"My poor family!" Mr. Washburn exclaimed. "Thomas was too hasty." He pulled his wife up and kissed her as the children rushed to hug him.

Esther picked Margaret up and soothed her until she stopped crying.

Mr. Washburn held up his hands for silence. "I'm terribly sorry you've all had such a scare," he said. Then he winced. "My foot."

Mrs. Washburn pulled Victoria and five-year-old Caleb away from him. "Mr. Washburn, do sit down," she said gently, drawing up a chair for him.

He dropped into it heavily and stared down at his bandaged right foot. "Thank you, Mrs. Washburn. And don't worry about my foot. It's only sprained."

"Father, please tell us what happened," Priscilla begged.

"A wagon that should have been passing me crashed into me," Mr. Washburn stated, half-grimly.

"Tell us more than that." Peter sat on the table and swung his legs, but at a motion from his mother, he slid to the floor.

Mr. Washburn shifted in his chair. "The accident happened half a mile from your uncle's place, beside that big hill right before the curve. I was thrown into the ditch, which sprained my foot and probably saved my life. The other team and wagon were all twisted up, and I could tell the driver was dead.

"The harness on my team was torn, so I hobbled over the hill to get to Thomas' house. Just when I'd reached the other side, I heard a horse stop beside the wagons. I turned back and recognized your uncle riding away in this direction. I shouted at him, but he didn't hear me. So I went on to his house where your aunt wrapped my foot and sent your cousins Dorothy and Reuben to get the team and wagon.

"She also insisted that I stay and rest a bit, so I did. When Thomas came home, he was so shocked to see me on his porch that he nearly fell off his horse. He gasped out that he'd told you I was dead, so I crawled onto the wagon and drove here as fast as I could."

Mr. Washburn glanced up and noticed Esther for the first time. "What are you doing over here, Esther?" he asked in surprise. "Don't tell me that my family has already spread the news of my death to the entire community." He turned from her to his wife with a look of alarm.

"No. We told the men who are going around collecting more soldiers for the army," Lydia spoke up. "They came after Uncle Thomas left, so we told them what we thought—that you were dead."

Mr. Washburn grinned. "A blessing in disguise! If those men think I am dead, they won't come back for me. I am sorry, though, that you had to worry about me."

Life is so unfair, Esther thought, biting her lip. "They took my father," she announced quietly.

Mr. Washburn stared at her.

"Those men took your father?" Mrs. Washburn asked.

Esther nodded, her arms tightening around Margaret.

"Oh, Esther, I'm so sorry." Lydia came over and hugged her.

Esther felt a tug on her dress and looked down. "What is it, Victoria?"

"I'll share my father with you." Victoria smiled shyly.

"That's kind of you, Victoria. Thank you." Esther squeezed her hand.

"Would you like to stay with us while your father is in the army, Esther?" Mrs. Washburn offered.

Esther shook her head. "I told Dad I would stay at home to take care of Milksop and Daisy. But I'll be sure to tell you if I need anything, and I'll come over when I get lonely."

Mrs. Washburn seemed to understand. "Of course, dear. You do whatever you think is best."

"Thank you. I don't know what I would do without you." Esther handed Margaret to Mrs. Washburn. "I should go home now, and I am so glad I don't need to return for a funeral." She smiled at Mr. Washburn.

He took a deep breath. "So am I."

18. News of Chancellorsville

That night Esther lit a candle and set it on her chest of draw-ers while she dressed for bed. She had combed her hair and was turning back her quilt when a gust of wind from the open window made the flame waver. Sitting on her bed, she watched it sputter out, leaving the room in darkness.

That can't happen to me, Esther thought, flopping back and staring upward. *I'm alone, but I must survive.*

The Washburns invited her over often, and she spent more time with them than she ever had before. Peter, Priscilla, Sarah, and Nicolas, the four oldest after Lydia, helped her spread hay-seed over the plowed field. Without her father there to help with the hoeing, she didn't want to plant corn. Hay only had to be planted and harvested, but corn had to be hoed all summer, and that was too much to ask of the Washburns.

Lydia, working four days a week at the General Store in town, promised to check the post office for letters from Esther's father. Close to the end of April, a week and a half after he was taken, she came over with a letter.

"This came for you today, Esther," she called, waving it above her head.

Esther put down the apron she was mending and ran down the porch steps. "Is it from Dad?"

"Yes. Open it." Lydia shoved the letter at her, breathing hard. "I want to know if he is all right."

Esther ripped the envelope open. She scanned the page and glanced back up with a smile. "He's all right, Lydia, and he sends your family his best."

Lydia beamed. "I'll be sure to tell them. I just stopped in to give you the letter. Good-bye."

She hurried along the path and disappeared into the woods. Esther returned to her chair on the porch and spread the letter on her lap.

Dear Esther,

The soldiers have been treating me well, so don't worry about me too much. We reached the army's headquarters yesterday afternoon, and I am sore from the long tramp. I don't know what company I am to be placed with, but maybe I can tell you in my next letter so you can write to me. Take care of the farm as well as you can. Whatever you decide to do, I know the Washburns will help you. Give them my best. I love you, and I am praying for you.

Your father,

Richard Sullivan

Esther stuck the letter back in the envelope and picked up her apron, stabbing the needle through the cloth in several half-hearted stitches. *Daddy, I miss you.*

Her thoughts spilled into words. "I wish you could come home." Heaving the apron away from her, she curled up in the chair, resting her chin on her knees as she gazed out over the tiny green shoots in the hayfield.

Esther tipped the heavy pot onto its side, spilling the dirty water on the grass. *I would take back all my complaints about this job if I could still be doing Dad's, David's, and Mama's washing,* she thought.

As she carried the wet clothes to the clothesline, she thought of the year before when David had come home to help with the spring planting. She was washing then too and had taken the last shirt from the line one afternoon when she felt something wet splatter across her back. Turning, she had found David standing behind her, his hand dripping and a grin on his face.

"Did you throw water on me?" she demanded.

His grin widened. "You mean that wasn't a wet bird flying over?" he asked innocently.

She frowned. "I know better than that, David. This"—she felt the wet spots on her back and pointed a finger at him—"came from you."

"Clever girl." He flicked his fingers at her again.

She wiped her cheeks with the dry shirt in her hand and dropped it into the basket. "I'm going to get you!" she said, lunging at him playfully.

He darted away from her, laughing. She chased him around the house without catching him, and when they went past the clothesline, she snatched up the basket of clothes and took it to the porch. When she turned around, he was waiting for her, dancing forward and backward on his toes. She slumped over and put her hands on her knees. He copied her, and they stared at each other, laughing breathlessly.

She rushed at him again, and he dodged away.

"Caught you!" she cried, touching his shirt.

"I didn't feel anything," he protested, and kept running. "I have to feel it."

Esther made a disgusted sound and plunged after him as he ran past the barn and headed for the field. Her legs felt wobbly, and her lungs seemed close to bursting. "How can you run so fast?" she panted.

David looked back over his shoulder and laughed. "It's all that drill I've been doing," he called. He reached the end of the field and started climbing the big rock at the edge of the woods.

Esther groaned and followed him. Hauling herself up onto the rock, she saw him jump off the other side. She scrambled across the top and jumped also. David rolled away and hopped up, but she grabbed his foot. He fell back to the ground with a yelp.

"I really caught...you this time!" she gasped, pressing a hand against her side.

He pulled his foot away from her and grinned. "Finally!"

They lay there for several minutes, and David said, "We sound like a couple of dogs, panting like this."

They both laughed—short, breathy laughs—and David sat up, pointing at her. "You are...crying, you are laughing so hard." He guffawed, slapping his leg.

Esther laughed even harder. Tears rolled down the side of her face into her ears, and she sat up to shake them out. "Enough laughing," she commanded weakly, wiping her eyes.

David grinned at her. "Your face is all red, and your hair is sticking up out of your braids."

She flopped back in the scratchy weeds. "I don't care. What were you doing up at the house? I thought you were helping Dad plant corn."

"I cut my hand on a rock." David held up his left hand, and she noticed for the first time that it was bandaged. "It wouldn't quit bleeding, so Dad told me to wrap it up."

"Is it deep?"

He shook his head. "Not really. It just bled a lot."

"I miss you so much when you are gone, David," Esther said after several minutes. "It's boring around here without you."

"I've missed you too, Little Birdie." David smiled at her. "I'm glad to be a part of the army, but I always look forward to coming home."

Esther sighed. "I should go back to the house and start supper."

"Yes, you should definitely do that." He nodded.

"And you"—she sat up and turned to him—"should go back to the field and reassure Dad that you haven't bled to death. He's likely wondering why you are taking so long."

David looked guilty. "I'll go at once." He jumped to his feet and pulled her up with him. "Would you like me to escort you to the house first?"

"Yes." Esther grinned at him. "But let's just walk."

So they had.

Remembering the happiness she'd felt that day, Esther sucked in a deep breath and thought she might start crying. David seemed closer to her than he had since she saw his face in the coffin.

Maybe Dad was right, that remembering helps, she thought. *But it won't bring him back.* She yanked one of her dresses out of the basket and started pinning it to the line.

Several days later Esther was outside shaking a rug when a team and wagon drove in the lane. It was Mr. Washburn and Lydia.

"Hello there," she called.

Lydia returned the greeting as Mr. Washburn pulled the horses to a halt and set the brake on the wagon. They both climbed down and came toward her. From their expressions she knew something was wrong.

"What is it?" she asked, her heart skipping a beat. "Not... Dad."

Lydia dropped her eyes, and Esther knew she was right.

"Tell me," she demanded, turning to Mr. Washburn. "What happened?"

Mr. Washburn cleared his throat. "There was a battle near Chancellorsville, Virginia, two days ago, Esther." He paused. "Your father is listed as missing in action."

The rug slipped from Esther's fingers as she sank to the step. "What does that mean?" she whispered.

Mr. Washburn shrugged. "It could mean one of several things," he said. "Either he was captured, or he was separated from his company and wounded too badly to find them again, in which case he might be permitted to return home to recover. And then again, it could mean that he was killed and they haven't found his body, or if they *have* found it, they were unable to identify—"

"Father, stop!" Lydia exclaimed, shocked.

Mr. Washburn looked at Esther, his blue eyes filling with remorse. "I'm sorry, Esther," he said. "That was thoughtless of me."

Esther shook her head and bit her lip as scenes from the hospital in Centreville swam in her mind. For a moment she could hardly breathe. *Oh, God, please don't do this to me,* she begged silently. *I need my dad.*

"If you want to come and live with us, you only have to say so." Lydia came to sit beside her and slipped an arm around her shoulders. "We would love to have you."

Esther nodded. "I know." She stood up and took a shaky breath. "Thank you for telling me about Dad, Mr. Washburn."

He nodded. "Esther, I am truly sorry." He handed her a letter. "This must have been posted before the battle."

"Thank you." Esther's voice broke when she saw "Pvt. Richard Sullivan" scrawled on the envelope in her father's handwriting. Underneath his name was an address similar to the one she had used when writing David, listing his company's initial and the brigade, division, and corps he was in. Her fingers trembled as she ripped open the envelope and pulled out the letter.

Dearest Esther,

I was placed with a company last week, and when I told my captain I wouldn't fight, he sent me to the major, who assigned me to take care of horses for the cavalry. It keeps me away from the rest of the men for the majority of the time, and most of the horses are fine animals. I have not seen Triangle since we arrived at headquarters and can only hope that she is being treated well.

The army is worse than I expected. I have heard about plans and campaigns for this summer, but nothing has happened yet, and the men are unmotivated. This war surely cannot go on much longer. David wasn't exaggerating when he complained about all the drilling. I haven't often been included, but the other new recruits are doing their share of it.

How are you getting along with the farm? I am almost glad I was taken before I planted the field, because you would've had a hard time raising corn by yourself. My advice would be to scatter some hayseed over whatever you can, because then you can at least put Milksop out to graze in it. If it has grown over with weeds already, don't feel badly. What is in the barn should last for another winter, and maybe by that time I will be home. I am glad, too, that we didn't get any of the Washburns' piglets last month. Maybe the next time they butcher a hog we can trade for some meat.

Write to me as soon as you can. I am anxious to hear how you are managing.

Your loving father,
Richard Sullivan

Esther sank to the step again and listened to the sound of the Washburn's wagon wheels fading in the distance. She stared at the envelope in her lap. *What if he never comes back? Will I live here alone forever without knowing what happened to him?*

His advice about what to plant in the field was comforting. *At least I did that right,* she thought.

That night she dreamed she was again following her father when he went outside to pray. From her position on the porch, she could see him as clearly as if it were day.

When he reached the rock, he shouted, "Oh, God, thank you for bringing me home!"

At his words, her heart beat faster, and she started to run toward him. She fell in the hayfield, landing hard, and lost sight of him.

"Dad! Daddy!" she called, panicking.

19. For David

Esther opened her eyes and found herself on the cold floor beside her bed. Scrambling to her feet, she went to the window and looked in the direction of the rock, almost believing she would see her father kneeling on it. But everything beyond the window-sill was shrouded in darkness.

"It was a dream," she whispered, turning away in disappointment. Then she remembered. He was missing in action.

"No!" she moaned. "I need him." She collapsed on her bed and curled into a ball, pulling her quilt over her. The house was eerily silent around her, and she shivered, squeezing her eyes shut against the blackness. *If only I knew what happened to him!*

"God, please be with me and show me what to do," she pleaded, her voice sounding small and scared in the emptiness. "I don't know why you allowed my dad to be taken, but I want to believe that you will take care of me while he is gone. And please take care of him too. Please let him be alive and let him come home. I know you can do that."

She took a deep breath and relaxed, convinced God had heard her prayer. The silence seemed comforting now, and the pounding of her heart slowed as she remembered part of the verse her father had given her.

Yea, in the shadow of thy wings will I make my refuge, until these calamities be overpast. She snuggled deeper under her quilt, reassured by the thought that God was holding her as she fell asleep.

Esther went to the Washburns the next day, taking the shortcut over the bridge that spanned the little creek in the woods. As she broke out of the trees and started toward the house, she heard a noise and turned to see Peter.

"Hello, Esther," he said in a soft voice. "I am really sorry about your dad."

Esther swallowed hard and nodded. "I am too."

"Are you going to come in?" Peter motioned toward the house. "Lydia has been anxious to see you. She's hoping you'll decide to come live with us." He peered at her, waiting for an answer.

I hate to disappoint Lydia, Esther thought. *Or any of them.* She didn't realize she had taken a step backward until Peter grabbed her wrist.

"Esther? What is the matter?"

She stared at him and pulled her hand away. "I've decided to stay at my house. But I hate to disappoint your family."

"Esther!" Peter rolled his eyes. "You are allowed to live wherever you want. Mother and Lydia might be disappointed, but you don't need to be afraid of telling them. They'll understand."

Why was I worried? Esther sighed and followed him to the house. "You're right."

He grinned at her. "Of course I am."

One month later at the beginning of June, Esther was working in her garden when she heard hoof beats coming up the road from town.

"Esther! Esther!"

Esther straightened up to see Lydia riding a white horse in the lane.

"Lovely! I do need a break." Esther stepped out of the row of carrots as the horse stopped beside the garden.

Lydia almost fell off in her haste to dismount. "Esther, look what came in the mail today," she said excitedly, holding out a thick envelope. "It's from your father!"

Esther dropped her hoe and grabbed the envelope, her heart beating faster as she saw her father's familiar handwriting. "Oh, yes!" she squealed. "It's from Dad! He's still alive!"

She hugged Lydia and spun around. "Lydia, thank you so much for bringing this out to me." She squinted past her friend to the white horse. "Where did you get that horse?"

Lydia grinned. "He was tied outside the store, and I begged permission from his owner to use him for a few minutes." She threw the reins over the horse's head and mounted. "I agreed to return at once or I would stay to see what your dad wrote."

Esther saw the longing on her face. "I'll come over tonight and tell you what he said," she promised. "All right?"

Lydia nodded. "Good-bye until then," she called, turning her horse's head toward the road. "I hope it is good news."

"So do I," Esther called after her, looking down at the envelope. "Thank you!"

She rushed to the house, and when she reached the cool dining room, she ripped open the envelope. Unfolding the letter, she found another one inside.

"To Captain Daniel Armstrong," she read, her forehead wrinkling.

She dropped it on the table and quickly scanned the first lines of her letter.

Dear Esther,

I was captured by the Confederates during the battle at Chancellorsville, and they are holding me in a prison in Petersburg, Virginia. It is not at all designed for the amount of people they have crammed into it, but I am managing. Do not try to write to me, because I think I might be taken to a different prison soon.

Esther sank into a chair. "At least he's alive," she whispered as she read on.

I have overheard from the guards that General Lee is planning to invade the north again and advance up the Cumberland Valley. Since the best connection we have in the army is Daniel Armstrong, I wrote to him, describing this information.

She glanced at the letter on the table.

The kindhearted guard who is standing in for the regular one gave me this paper and promised to mail my letter to you, but I didn't think he would want to mail my letter to Daniel, so I put it inside yours. And I don't know if I'll be able to write you any more letters, because the regular guard is very hostile to us Northern prisoners. But I will try.

I've been thinking about you a lot, Esther. If you are still living on the farm rather than with the Washburns, you must be terribly lonely. What if you would go to the army and volunteer as a nurse in a field hospital unit? Doctor Anderson said you would make an excellent nurse, remember? David would be glad you haven't given up on helping others, just because you weren't able to save him. You could take my letter to Daniel yourself instead of mailing it. Once you get there, you'll probably find some other women who are volunteering as nurses and can stay with them.

I am sure the Washburns would be glad to care for Milksop and Daisy and look after our farm while you are gone.

I love you, Esther, and I will pray every day that God
will keep you safe. God has promised to hear and answer
our prayers, even before we ask him. Never forget that.
Remember that verse in Psalms, and no matter what happens, trust in God and rest in the shadow of his wings.

Thinking of you always, your father,

Richard Sullivan

Esther reread the letter, her mind churning. *Go to the army
and be a volunteer nurse? Could I? Or should I just send this letter to
Daniel? I wonder how soon General Lee plans to invade Pennsylvania.*

"Oh, bother!" she said aloud, borrowing David's custom-
ary complaint. "I wish General Lee would go back where he
came from and leave us all in peace. I wish this war was over
and Dad could come home." She sighed and went upstairs to
her room.

Pulling open her top drawer, she stared at the collection of
things inside. Her mother's necklace was still there, along with
Highland Rose, the facedown plaque of Triangle, dozens of letters, and David's uniform. She put her father's letter in with the
others and lifted out her brother's coat, fingering the worn, dark-
blue cloth. He'd worn it home but had said he didn't want it
anymore, so she'd washed and mended it before tucking it into
her odds-and-ends drawer.

Unfolding it, Esther slipped her arms into the coat sleeves.
The gold bars on the shoulders sparkled as they caught the light,
and she remembered the first time she had seen them when
David came home for Christmas. Memories of the good times
they had spent together during those few days flooded her mind,
and she winced.

Dropping on her bed, she cried, "Oh, God, why does it have
to hurt so much? I can't seem to think about him without getting
upset at you for taking him away."

Her father had told her Doctor Cunningham said no one could have prevented David's death. *But I still wish I could have done something more.*

She took off the blue coat. *If I go to the army and be a nurse, like Dad suggested, I'll be able to do something more for a lot of men like him.*

Folding the coat, she put it back in her top drawer. "I'll do it, Dad," she said aloud. "For David."

20. An Angel

That evening, Esther walked over to tell the Washburns about her father's letter. As she passed the barn, ten-year-old Jacob jumped out from behind the watering trough and roared at her.

She shook her head and smiled. "I saw you, Jacob. Your knee was showing."

He snickered, running ahead of her to the house.

Lydia caught her inside the door and squeezed her hands. "What did the letter say?" she asked eagerly.

Esther glanced up as the rest of the family gathered around. "Dad was captured during the battle at Chancellorsville and taken to a prison in Petersburg, Virginia," she told them. "He overheard from the guards that General Lee plans to invade the North by way of the Cumberland Valley, and he wanted to inform our side, so he wrote a letter to David's captain.

"But he didn't think his guard would mail it for him, so he put it in my letter. I'm going to take it to him and then stay with a field hospital unit and be a volunteer nurse."

"You're going to the army?" Peter exclaimed. "That's not fair. You get to go everywhere. First Manassas and now the army. I wish I could go somewhere."

Esther laughed. "Manassas and the army is everywhere?"

"Of course not." Priscilla crossed her eyes at Peter. "Silly boy."

He returned the face.

"It won't be easy, and I'll miss you all terribly," Esther continued, looking around at them. "But I'm doing it for David."

Mrs. Washburn nodded. "I understand, Esther. I think you'll make a wonderful nurse."

Lydia sighed. "Oh, Esther. I think so too, and I'm happy you'll be able to help the wounded, but I sure will miss you."

Esther hugged her. "I'll miss all of you too, but I'm not leaving for a couple more days, so don't say good-bye yet."

She glanced at Mr. and Mrs. Washburn. "Will you take care of Milksop and Daisy and look after my garden? I didn't plant much, but it shouldn't be wasted."

They looked at each other, and then Mr. Washburn nodded. "Of course," he said. "You can bring your animals over the night before you leave."

Esther smiled at him. "All right. Thank you."

After an entire morning of wondering what she could pack her clothes in, Esther remembered David's haversack. They had brought it back from Centreville, and she went to the closet beside her room to look for it. *This should work,* she decided when she'd found it. *And I can use his bedroll and canteen too, after I wash them.*

David's knife was at the bottom of the haversack, and she left it there, putting her clothes on top of it. She baked some bread and other food and packed it into the haversack with portions of flour, cornmeal, dried beans, salted pork, and seasoning herbs.

Late the next afternoon, she heard a knock on the door. Glancing out the window, she saw Peter rocking back and forth on his heels as he waited for her to answer his knock. She grinned and opened the door. "Hello, Peter."

He stared at her, tapping his fingers against the doorframe. "I forgot why I came! Oh, no, I remember now. Mother sent me to ask if you can come over for supper, since you're leaving tomorrow."

"Of course I'll come!" Esther smiled, delighted. "I won't have to worry about making supper."

"Yes, that's exactly what Mother said. See you tonight." He catapulted off the porch.

Esther enjoyed every minute she spent with the Washburns that evening, knowing it would be a long time until she saw them again. Victoria and Sarah wanted to sit beside her during supper, and she held Margaret most of the evening. When she went home, Lydia and the twins went with her as far as the bridge in the woods.

"I'll miss you, Esther," Lydia said, hugging her.

Esther squeezed her hand. "I'll miss you too, Lydia," she said. "You and Priscilla are my best friends."

"Can you imagine?" Priscilla broke in. Her voice quivered. "I think *I* am even going to miss you."

Peter sniffed. "Pull yourself together, 'Cilla," he commanded. "I hope you won't take it upon yourself to miss me, Esther. I'm not worth the trouble."

"Peter!" Lydia exclaimed.

Esther laughed at her expression. "I'm not sure I can help myself, Peter," she said, turning away. "Good-bye, all of you."

"Good-bye," they called after her.

The next morning Esther pulled on a faded green dress and wrapped her braids around her head. Carrying her bedroll, canteen, and haversack downstairs, she went to the kitchen and finished the last of the cold ham and bread she'd eaten for lunch the day before.

Stepping out onto the porch, she noticed the sun's first rays filtering through the distant trees. She sighed, glancing at the barn, the fields, and the little clearing where her mother and David had been buried. Without the rest of her family, her home felt so empty that she was almost glad to be leaving.

Slinging the haversack, bedroll, and canteen over her shoulder, she started up the road toward Kirksville.

"The last I heard, the army was somewhere in Maryland or Virginia," she thought aloud. "So if I go east to Chambersburg and then travel south, like we did when we went to Manassas to get David, I should find it sooner or later. And I can always ask someone."

She stopped at noon to eat and rest, shifting the haversack's straps back and forth between her shoulders. *Oh, bother!* she complained to herself. *I didn't realize how heavy this would get!*

By the end of the day, Esther's feet and legs ached. Hearing water a short distance away, she left the road and found a little stream. The secluded grassy clearing would be a good place to spend the night, and she spread her bedroll, sitting down with a sigh.

She tried to calculate how many miles she'd walked but gave up after a moment. Pulling off her shoes and stockings, she dangled her feet in the cool water and took a piece of cheese from her haversack to munch on.

I don't know if I can keep this up, she thought wearily. Drying her feet, she climbed into her bedroll, listening to the water tumble over the rocks as she drifted to sleep.

It took her six days to reach Chambersburg. The walking grew easier, but she was still tired when she collapsed on her bedroll at the end of each day. Once when she passed through a town, she replenished her store of food. Before he was drafted, her father had told her where to find the money he kept for emergencies, and she had brought some of it along.

In Chambersburg she turned south on the road that led to Hagerstown, Maryland. After traveling for three days, she had crossed the border into Maryland and knew she should find out for sure where the army was. *I'll ask the next person I meet,* she promised herself.

A wagon had passed her that morning, and she came upon it again well after noon. The horses were tied to a tree beside the road, and the driver was lying down in the shade. As she approached, the man stood up and began to untie his team.

She took a deep breath, blurting out the question before she lost her courage. "Sir, do you know where the army of the Potomac is camped right now?"

As he stopped fumbling with the reins and looked up, she noticed that most of his right arm was missing. His forehead wrinkled. "And what would you be wanting with the army, lassie?"

Esther smiled, fascinated by his Scottish accent. "I'm on my way to deliver a message to my brother's captain," she told him. "And then I'm going to work as a volunteer nurse in a field hospital unit."

A wide grin split the man's face. "Are ye now," he said. "That is wonderful! And I just heard that the army will be camping near the town of Fredrick. Come, I'll take ye there myself."

"Will you?" Esther rubbed her shoulder under the haversack strap. "I am so tired of walking."

The man shrugged, smoothing his flaxen beard. "Anything to help our army," he said. The way he trilled his r's reminded her of a bird. "I wanted to enlist, but they said I should try to serve my country in other ways." He smiled at her, his green eyes twinkling. "Like giving rides to young lasses who are delivering messages and wanting to be nurses."

Esther smiled back at him. "Thank you, sir. You are an answer to my prayer."

He nodded. "God looks after his children, he does. Come, lass, let us be off." He climbed into the wagon, laid the reins across his knee, and reached down to help her up.

She sank onto the hard seat beside him, thankful for the chance to rest her aching legs. The wagon was empty except for some hay, and she dropped her haversack and bedroll into a corner. The miles went by much faster under the horses' feet than they had under her own, and when it grew dark, they stopped for the night.

"We should reach Fredrick tomorrow afternoon," the man told her, setting the brake on the wagon before jumping to the ground.

Esther helped him unhitch the horses and offered to cook supper if he made a fire. She had noticed cooking utensils and food under the wagon seat.

The Scotsman took one bite of her cabbage stew and grinned. "With making food like this, lass, it'll be a lucky man who gets to spend his life with you. I haven't had such tasty cabbage since me wife died."

Esther couldn't stop the giggle that bubbled up inside her. "That's very kind of you to say," she told him. "It's been a long time since I cooked for someone other than myself." She sighed.

"A long time, you say?" He scooped a piece of cornbread from the iron skillet. "Would you like to tell me about it?" He glanced at her. "I'll tell you how I lost me arm."

Esther smiled a little, suddenly realizing that she wanted to tell him. *If his wife died, he'll understand how I feel.*

"My mother died two years ago," she said slowly, staring into the dancing flames between them. "From influenza. My brother enlisted shortly after her funeral. He was wounded at the Second Battle of Bull Run. We brought him home, but he—" She stopped, unable to get another word past the lump in her throat.

"Did he die too, lass?"

The man's voice was gentle, and when Esther looked up and saw the compassion in his green eyes, the lump in her throat grew until she thought it might choke her. She nodded.

"What about your father?" he asked quietly.

Esther swallowed hard and took a long, shaky breath. "He was drafted after that awful law was passed, and then he was captured at Chancellorsville. He wrote me from a prison in Petersburg three weeks ago, so he was alive then, at least."

"I'm so sorry, lass."

Esther heard his voice break and looked up to see tears in his eyes. "You have suffered much," he said. "Let me tell you how I lost me wife, and me arm."

He sniffed and rubbed his nose. "Tara, she was helping me cut down a tree on our farm, seven months past our wedding. When the tree started falling, I saw that it would land right between us, so I shouted for her to stay where she was. A branch broke off and knocked me to the ground, crushing my arm."

He paused, seeming to relive the moment. "She would not have been killed if she had stayed where she was. But she came running to help me, and the tree fell on her. I have been alone for eight years now, I have."

Esther felt a lump in her throat again as he fell silent. "I'm sorry, sir. I cannot imagine losing someone in that way."

He nodded. "I cannot imagine losing so many of the ones I love in so short a time. So we're even, we are."

Taking more stew, he began to eat it. Esther stared at the fire. "Does it ever stop hurting?" she asked quietly.

He studied her for a moment, his eyes sad. "No, lass. Me heart still longs after Tara. But me hurt over losing her is not so fierce now."

He smiled at her. "You are tired, I see. Would you like to sleep under the wagon? I can wash the pans and sleep under the tree beside me horses."

Esther nodded. "Thank you."

She rolled herself up in her bedroll under the wagon, repeating his words in her mind. *Me hurt over losing her is not so fierce now.* It reminded her of what her father had told her about David not long ago. "*We've finally started to get over losing him, but we still need each other.*"

"Dear God," she whispered, "please keep Dad alive and safe until he can come home."

A pale sliver of the moon hung above the trees when they set off the next morning well after dawn. As the sun climbed higher, it faded. The rest of the day was hot, and the sky shimmered above them in an unbroken expanse of blue. It was almost evening by the time they reached Fredrick, and Esther shifted on the wagon seat, sore from so much sitting.

She could see the white tents of the encampment long before they actually arrived. When they topped a hill, she caught her breath as she saw the scene spread out in the valley before them. *There are so many tents, and so many soldiers!* A dart of fear pierced her confidence. *How will I ever find Daniel?*

The streets were crowded as they drove into Fredrick, and Esther's heart sank. *It might take me weeks just to find out where the Third Corps is*, she thought in despair.

"Here we are. This is Fredrick." The man turned to her. "Where are you needing to go?"

Esther hesitated. "Do you know where the army has its headquarters?" she asked. "If you take me there, I can ask someone where my brother's captain's company is camped."

The man nodded. "They're using the brick building there, see?" He pointed to a house at the end of the street and pulled the horses to a halt when they reached it.

Climbing down from the wagon, she took her bedroll, haversack, and canteen from the wagon bed. "Thank you so much, sir," she said, turning to face him. "I'm not sure what I would have done without you."

He shrugged. "A smart lass like you would have managed on her own. But I was honored to be of service."

He is so kind! A thought crashed into Esther's mind, and she blurted, "Are you an angel?"

He snorted. "No, lass. Angels don't have green eyes."

Her eyes widened. He spoke as though green eyes were the worst kind to have. "How do you know?" she demanded. "And besides, I like your eyes."

"You do?"

When she nodded, he smiled, taking up the reins in his one hand. "Good day, lassie."

Esther watched him drive off. *Thank you for sending him to me, God,* she thought. *Telling him about my family made me feel better, and riding with him saved me several days of walking. Now I just need to find Daniel's company.*

A lieutenant at the army's headquarters gave her directions to the Third Corps' First Division, but the sun was slipping behind the horizon when she finally reached the Second Brigade. After passing the tents of five other companies, she asked a soldier from company H if she was at all close to Company K.

"It's right on the other side of that clump of maples, miss," he told her.

Relieved, she headed for the trees, suddenly noticing how dark it was. *Maybe I should find a place to spend the night and wait until morning to find Daniel.*

Esther spread her bedroll beside one of the biggest maples and hoped she wouldn't be in anyone's way. She was too tired to move.

The sun had already risen by the time Esther awoke, and she hurriedly folded up her bedroll. She wet a corner of her dress from her canteen and washed her face. Digging through her haversack, she pulled out her wooden comb. Taking down her hair, she combed and re-braided it, and as she wrapped her braids around her head, she wished for her looking glass.

She stepped out of the trees and saw a posted board beside the circle of tents proclaiming, "Company K, 99th Pennsylvania Vols.," in crude charcoal lettering. A lone soldier sprawled by a tent, whittling on a stick of wood, and a group of men sat near another tent.

Esther headed toward the whittling soldier, hoping he could tell her where Daniel was. "Sir?"

He stopped digging at his stick and squinted up at her.

She took a deep breath to steady her voice. "Do you know where can I find Captain Armstrong?"

"Cap'n Armstrong?" He leaned back on his elbow to squint up at her again. "I dunno. Ask the lieutenant."

The lieutenant? Esther searched her memory for the name of the soldier who stepped up when her brother resigned. *It was Jack something,* she told herself. *Jack Mayden? No. Manden? No, not that either. Mason! That was it.*

"Lieutenant Jack Mason?" she asked, pleased that she remembered.

"Yep. Him or anybody else."

"Where can I find the lieutenant?" Esther persisted.

"He's over there playing cards." The soldier jerked his chin in the direction of the group of men. "He's near the center... Oh, there. He stood up."

Esther felt relieved. "Thank you, sir," she said as he went back to his whittling.

Hurrying to catch up with the lieutenant, Esther followed him away from the other men. "Lieutenant Mason?" she said. "Lieutenant Jack Mason?"

The young man stopped walking and turned. "Yes?" he said courteously. "What can I do for you?"

She swallowed, hoping she didn't look as unsure of herself as she felt. "Where can I find Captain Daniel Armstrong?"

"Oh. You…" Lieutenant Jack Mason scratched his head. "Captain Armstrong is not here right now. What do you need?"

"I have a message for him," Esther explained.

"A message?" Jack scratched his head again. "I don't know when he'll be back. Shall I relay your message to him when he returns?"

Esther shook her head. "I'm supposed to deliver it in person."

Jack nodded, shrugging. "You can wait for him under that tree."

Esther walked over to sit down under the enormous maple he had motioned to. Leaning back against the trunk, she looked up at the green leaves, remembering how she'd told the Scottish man that he was an answer to her prayer.

An answer to what prayer? she asked herself, closing her eyes. *Maybe Dad's prayer.* She smiled.

The day was warm, but a cool breeze stirred the leaves above her, and somewhere a wren was singing. The men by the tents argued over their game of cards, and the wren's cheerful song rippled through the air.

Esther felt calmer than she had since leaving home. *I'm glad God is looking out for me.*

Hearing footsteps, she opened her eyes and saw Jack Mason. "The captain is coming, miss," he said, stopping a few feet away.

"Thank you." Esther scrambled to her feet and smoothed the wrinkles from her light brown dress. She saw Daniel coming past the tents and touched her braids. For the second time that day, she wished for her looking glass.

21. Valuable Information?

Daniel stopped beside Jack. "Esther? You are the last person I expected to see here."

"Hello, Daniel," Esther said slowly, deciding not to curtsy.

Jack nodded to both of them and walked toward the tents.

Daniel blinked and then a quick smile dissolved his startled expression. "Forgive me, Esther. Shall we walk?" He motioned to some distant trees. "Or would you rather sit?"

"Walking is fine." Esther took a few steps and glanced at him. "I brought you a message."

"Jack told me. Esther—" Daniel paused, and she looked up at him. "I am so sorry about David."

Esther felt her chest tighten. "Dad must have written you," she said, staring at the ground.

"Yes. After the funeral," he said quietly. "He said David would've wanted me to know."

Yes, he would have. Esther tried to swallow.

"I never had a better friend in the army," Daniel said. "I miss him every day, and I only met him a couple years ago. When I heard, I was glad I was not you or your father."

Esther snuck a quick glance at his face and saw unmistakable sadness there.

"And yet," Daniel went on, "you have so many better memories of him than I do." He stopped walking and gave her a wry grin. "So now I am rather envious. Your loss was much greater than mine, but so was your gain."

Esther turned and stared at him for a long moment. "I never thought of it like that," she whispered. "Thank you."

He seemed surprised. "You're welcome." Looking away, he shoved his hands in his pockets and started walking again. "What is your message?"

"Oh." Esther followed him, pulling her father's letter from her pocket. "It's from Dad."

He looked at her strangely as he took it. "What happened to him?"

Her eyes darted to his. "He's in prison in Petersburg, Virginia," she said slowly. "He didn't think they would mail a letter to an army captain, so he put it inside a letter to me."

"What happened before the Confederate prison?" Daniel asked, unfolding the paper. "Did your father abandon his beliefs, or was he drafted?"

Esther felt a sudden surge of anger. "He was drafted, of course!" She started walking back toward the tents.

Daniel caught up with her before she'd gone far. "You've had a rough time, Esther. I wish I could say something more comforting than I'm sorry."

Esther relaxed. "Was his information of any value?"

"It would've been three weeks ago." Daniel sighed, stuffing the letter into his pocket. "But not now. I'm sorry you came all this way for nothing."

Esther shrugged. "I didn't figure the letter would be worth much. Walking here took me too long."

"Who's taking care of your farm?"

"The Washburns. I took Milksop and Daisy over to their pasture before I left."

"Milksop." Daniel wrinkled his forehead. "Isn't that your cow?"

She nodded, surprised. "Yes, and Daisy is her two-month-old heifer."

He grinned. "I remembered, because that's not a word you usually find attached to a cow."

Esther laughed a little. "I know." She flushed, not about to tell him that she'd been the one to come up with it.

"Don't you also have a horse?" he questioned. "It had a strange name too."

"Triangle." Just thinking about it made Esther upset. "Those recruiting men took her when they took Dad."

"Oh." Daniel grimaced. "The army took a lot from you, Esther Sullivan."

Esther glanced at him and led the way to the trees where she had spent the night. "There's another reason I came," she said, grabbing her haversack, bedroll, and canteen. "I want to work as a nurse. I can't stand the silence at my house, and I want to help others like I helped David." She bit her lip and looked down for a moment. "Do you know of any field hospital units that have women nurses I could stay with?"

He shook his head.

Her shoulders slumped, and he said quickly, "Not right off, that is. But I'm sure I can find you one. Would you like to help with the wounded soldiers in my regiment's hospital tent until I find some women for you to stay with?"

Esther hesitated and then nodded.

"I'll take you there now." Daniel held out his hand. "Shall I carry your things?"

"Yes, thank you." Esther passed them over and followed him.

When they reached the hospital tent, he told the doctor in charge that she wanted to help with the wounded.

"An assistant!" the doctor exclaimed, his tired face lighting up. "Just what I need."

"I'll check around with the field hospital units and come back when I've found some women for you to stay with," Daniel told her. "You'll be all right here?"

"I'll be fine," Esther said, but her heart sank. Daniel was the only person she knew in the entire army.

He flashed her an encouraging smile. "Good-bye for now, then."

22. Sniper

The doctor showed Esther what to do without saying much, and she noticed dark circles under his eyes. *The doctors are wearing themselves out,* she thought sadly. *Will there ever be an end to the wounded?*

She rolled up her sleeves and began washing dirty dishes, feeding hungry men, and dressing wounds.

Late that afternoon Daniel came back with good news. "There are two women with the Second Corps field hospital unit," he explained, as Esther followed him out of the tent she'd been working in. "I didn't meet them, but the doctor said they have their own tent and are helping him with the wounded."

They reached the Second Corps field hospital unit only after they'd walked through what Esther felt sure was the entire camp. She raised her eyebrows at Daniel as they passed tent after tent, as if to say, "I hope you know where you're going."

He responded with a lazy grin. "The doctor said the nurses' tent was all the way at the end."

When they reached the last one, he called out a brief hello and then added, "May I speak to the nurse in charge?"

This tent was much smaller than the others. The door flaps were tied back, and Esther saw a woman inside bending over a cot. She straightened and came toward them.

"I am the only nurse here right now," she said. Her face lit up as her eyes met Esther's. "A girl! How lovely." She came forward and engulfed Esther in a brief hug. "I don't get to see many girls. Is there something I can do for you?"

Daniel touched the brim of his hat. "Captain Armstrong, ma'am."

"Is this your sister, Captain?" A strand of frizzy golden hair fell across the nurse's brown eyes as she tilted her head toward Esther. "Although I must say, you don't look a bit like each other. Is she your wife?"

Esther stared at the young woman and threw a glance at Daniel, her eyes widening. *Does she assume every man and woman she sees together are either siblings or man and wife?*

Daniel grinned his lazy grin at the nurse. "You're rushing to conclusions, ma'am," he drawled. "We're just friends. Her brother was my first lieutenant, and that's how we met."

"I want to be a volunteer nurse," Esther blurted, not sure what else Daniel might say. "May I stay with you?"

The young woman blinked. "Of course you may, dear. We can't let you stay with the soldiers. But do you have any experience? It's hard work."

"Yes, I know," Esther said. "I helped a doctor with the wounded from the Second Battle of Bull Run."

The young woman nodded. "So you do know what it's like. By the way, my name is Agnes Whitaker. Please call me Agnes."

Esther smiled. "I am Esther Sullivan."

Agnes beamed at her. "What a pretty name! Come, I'll show you our tent."

She led them inside. A sheet curtained off one corner, and there were four wounded men on cots in the first part.

Agnes slipped behind the sheet and held it back for them to follow her as she said, "This is where we nurses sleep. Since there is never enough room in the other tents for the wounded, we are using some of the space in our tent."

Daniel turned slightly, glancing at the two cots along the side of the tent. "Miss Whitaker, is there another nurse that stays here with you?"

"Yes, an older woman. Florence Ryan." Agnes' smile looked a little strained. "She likes helping the men, but sometimes she can be cantankerous. Don't worry, though," she added, turning to Esther. "She won't mind at all if you stay with us."

"Will she be safe with you and Miss Ryan?" Daniel took off his hat, running his fingers through his hair. "Her father asked me to keep an eye on her if she decided to come be a nurse." He turned to Esther. "In his letter."

"He did?" Esther raised her eyebrows and suddenly pictured her father sitting in prison. *He'll never stop looking out for me,* she realized, and the reminder of his love made her smile. Her heart ached for him.

Agnes tucked the frizzy strand of hair behind her ear. "Don't you worry, Captain Armstrong," she said. "We'll look after your friend."

Daniel replaced his hat. "Thank you, Miss Whitaker. I should get back to my men now."

Agnes nodded, curtsying when he tipped his hat. "Good-bye, Captain."

Esther curtsied too, smiling at him. "Good-bye, Daniel. Thank you for finding a place for me to stay."

He waved his hand. "Don't mention it."

Esther immediately started helping Agnes take care of wounded soldiers. At the end of the day when she dropped onto the cot they'd found for her, she was worn out. Florence, the older nurse who slept in their tent, came in after Esther was asleep and left almost before she was up, so she didn't see much of her. Florence seemed to enjoy working by herself, unlike Agnes, who always tried to be in the same tent as Esther.

Two days later the army marched north, and so did the Second Corps field hospital unit. Only the soldiers who couldn't walk or were otherwise seriously injured were still with them, riding in the ambulance and two other wagons. The rest had rejoined their regiments.

At the end of the third day, they pitched their tents on Pennsylvania soil. The next day the order to advance didn't come until well after noon. Esther asked Agnes why they had to keep moving the wounded men, and Agnes said she didn't like it either but there was nothing they could do about it.

"Some Union soldiers fought the Confederates only a few miles from here yesterday, close to the town of Gettysburg," Agnes continued. "We have to go farther northeast until we're close enough to help the wounded yet far enough away that we're not in danger."

Esther helped Agnes take down their tent and pack it into one of their unit's wagons. Several of the men had left to go home the day before, so the wounded all fit into the ambulance wagon. They set off down a dirt road. An hour later Esther, riding in the bed of the last wagon, shifted on her bedroll.

Oh, dear. She glanced ahead to where Agnes was driving another wagon. *Why didn't she stop me from drinking so much water this morning? I can't ask the whole procession to stop on my account. Maybe I can be back before anyone notices that I'm gone.*

She jumped over the side of the slow-moving wagon, trying to land on her feet but tumbling forward into the grass. Clambering to her feet, she hurried into the scraggly brush that lined the road.

Esther was breathless when she reappeared, wishing she wouldn't have taken so long. The road was empty, the wagons gone.

She ran up the road. But when she rounded a bend and still couldn't see anything, she stopped. "Am I going the right way?" she wondered aloud, pressing a hand against her throbbing side.

Turning, she started back the way she had come. It was cloudy, so she couldn't get her bearings from the sun. She heard hoof beats coming toward her and soon saw a black horse cantering up the road, two soldiers in blue uniforms on its back.

The horse looked familiar, somehow. She stared harder. *It's Raven!* she realized with a surge of relief. "Daniel!" she called, waving her arm as she backed off the road.

It didn't look like they were going to stop, and she wondered if they'd even heard her. But Daniel must have, because as they passed her, Raven slowed and turned, prancing to a halt.

Esther smiled up at them, wondering what Daniel and Jack were both doing away from their men. She had never been so glad to see anyone in her entire life.

"Esther, you're heading the wrong direction," Daniel said, swinging his right leg forward over Raven's neck.

Frowning, Jack dismounted also.

"I got separated from my wagon," Esther said regretfully, "and now I'm lost."

"You can come with us," Daniel spoke quickly. "Mason and I will hold the stirrups and run alongside as you ride."

Esther heard Jack mumble something about already being late as he walked to the other side of Raven. Daniel held out his hand to help her up, and she noticed a movement beyond him on the other side of the road.

Her heart nearly stopped. A Confederate soldier stepped out of the trees and raised his gun, aiming it at Daniel.

23. Rock Creek

"Daniel, move!" Esther shrieked. She jumped forward and shoved Daniel's shoulders, pushing him backward.

He stumbled and sprawled on the ground as the gray-uniformed soldier fired his gun. Esther felt a searing sensation in her right arm and fell to her knees with a jolt. She gasped for air and couldn't get any. Slumping over, she gazed up at the sky, wondering if she was going to die.

Then air whooshed into her lungs, and she rolled over, bumping into Daniel. He was crouching, scanning the road. The Confederate had stepped behind a tree to reload but was still visible. Daniel pulled out the small pistol tucked in his belt and cocked it.

"No!" Esther cried, knocking the gun from his hand.

It skittered on the road, and Jack darted from behind Raven. He picked up the pistol and fired toward the trees.

Esther heard a cry and sat up, looking to where the Confederate had been. Daniel moved in front of her and helped her up.

"Come, Esther. Let's get you away from here."

"Daniel!" she cried. "Don't touch my arm!"

She pulled away and cradled it with her good hand. There was a jagged hole in her sleeve, and blood was starting to ooze out. She looked away, feeling dizzy. She felt Daniel holding her shoulder before she realized she was swaying.

"Mason!" he called. "She's hit! Bring Raven here." He motioned to where the black horse now stood beside the road.

Jack started toward them. "Captain, we need to leave!" He grabbed Raven's reins and led him over.

Daniel held out the stirrup for Esther, glancing down at her. She took a deep breath and felt blood trickle through the fingers holding her injured arm.

"I can do it," she whispered. "I'll be all right."

She reached for Raven's mane and fell against the horse. Daniel grimaced and lifted her up onto the saddle.

"Thank you." Esther grabbed Raven's reins with her good hand.

"Come on, Captain," Jack griped. "We've had to leave behind wounded civilians before. Can't we just go?"

"Shut up, Mason. She is David's sister. Hold the stirrup and run."

"Really? The one who sent him cookies? I thought she reminded me of someone."

Esther felt Jack looking at her with profound respect as he took his place on the other side of the horse. Daniel spoke to Raven, and they started off. Esther's arm throbbed with each step, and she gritted her teeth.

Fortunately, less than a mile down the road Daniel stopped his horse and pointed to a group of Union soldiers marching not far away.

"Mason," he said breathlessly, "there's our company. You will take charge of the men while I take Miss Sullivan to her hospital unit."

"Why can't you let her go by herself?" Jack demanded, panting. "She's not hurt that badly."

"He's right," Esther said, starting to slide off. "I'll be fine." Her feet hit the ground, and she crumpled, groaning.

"Go on, Mason," she heard Daniel say. "Just hold the men together until I get back. I shouldn't be long."

"All right, I'll do it," Jack muttered. "For David's sake, if nothing else."

Daniel helped Esther to her feet and pulled her hand off her injured arm. "Don't touch it," he instructed. "You'll make it worse."

She glared at him, her eyes watering with the pain. "How can I make it worse?" She clamped her hand back over the wound.

Daniel yanked her hand away again. "I told you not to touch it." His voice was sharp, and he pressed her fingers until she stopped fighting his grip and looked up at him. "If you squeeze it like that, the bullet might explode and rip up more of your arm," he explained.

"Oh." She felt exhausted. "Then I'll try not to do it again."

"Let's go. I heard that the hospital unit was setting up near Rock Creek." Daniel helped her up behind the saddle and then put his left foot in the stirrup, throwing his right leg over Raven's neck.

They rode in silence for a few minutes, and then he asked, "Why didn't you want me to shoot that Rebel soldier? He shot you."

Esther didn't answer right away. She couldn't tell him how she really felt without sounding disrespectful. "I reacted without thinking," she said at last and then lied. "I'm sorry."

He nodded, and she shuddered, trying not to think of how many more men would be killed that day, how many Daniel would kill. She never wanted to see another person die.

The throbbing of Esther's arm increased with every jolt of Raven's hooves. She bit her lip until she tasted blood. Before they had gone a mile, her head pounded relentlessly.

A shot rang out in the distance, followed by an explosion of other guns and cannons.

The battle! Esther thought dizzily. The roaring of countless guns thudded in every joint of her body.

Daniel urged Raven to a canter, and they rode another mile before Esther caught sight of the ambulance and other supply wagons in the distance. The pounding in her head had increased, and the tents seemed blurry.

She grabbed Daniel's arm, and he shifted to look at her, reaching back with his arm to steady her. He called her name and pulled on the reins, but his voice sounded far away. Raven slowed, and Esther slumped forward.

Everything went dark.

24. After the Battle

Esther felt herself being carried and tried to blink away the fog in her eyes. Her head throbbed from the pain in her arm and the incessant gunfire that filled the air.

"Miss Whitaker!" she heard Daniel call.

Esther looked up, gripping his arm with her good hand. Daniel glanced down at her, and she saw relief in his brown eyes.

"Esther, what is wrong?" Agnes rushed toward them. "Your arm! Captain Armstrong, what happened?"

"A sniper's bullet." Daniel scowled. "Meant for me."

"A bullet!" Agnes's voice was horrified. "Esther, what were you doing on the battlefield?"

"I wasn't," Esther muttered, wishing Agnes would stop talking so loudly. "It was only one solitary Confederate. I think I can stand now, Daniel."

He set her gently on her feet. "Miss Whitaker, can you take out the bullet, or shall I find a doctor?"

Agnes looked doubtful. "I'll try," she promised. "But I might only make it worse."

She pulled a cot from a nearby wagon and started setting it up. Esther moved toward it and stumbled. She gasped as pain shot through her arm. Blood was seeping from the bullet hole, staining her blue dress dark red.

Daniel caught her elbow. "Careful now."

Esther concentrated on staying upright for several more steps. She reached the cot at last and lay down on it. Agnes pushed her bloody sleeve out of the way and began to probe the wound with her finger.

"I'm sorry, Esther," she murmured. "This isn't going to be easy for you."

Esther's vision swam, and the pain increased until she was sure she would die. She cried out in spite of her resolve not to. Daniel crouched beside her and held out his hand.

"Here, Esther," he offered. "You can squeeze my hand when it hurts."

Esther nodded and felt his fingers close over hers. Agnes probed deeper, and fiery pain shot up her arm. She gripped Daniel's hand with all her might and tried to hold still. Blackness started to rush in again, but then it was over.

Agnes held up the bullet with a look of amazement. "You are lucky it didn't burst, Esther," she said. "Most bullets explode on contact. And it wasn't that deep, either. You were fortunate."

Daniel released Esther's hand and stood up, wiping his forehead on his sleeve. "Thank you, Miss Whitaker," he said. "I will come back after the battle to see how she is doing."

"Don't worry, Captain," Agnes reassured him. "We'll take good care of her, I promise."

"I'm sure you will. Don't let her off that cot, and Esther, mind Miss Whitaker." He shook his finger at her.

"Are you trying to look fatherly?" Esther mumbled.

Agnes giggled as Daniel tipped his cap. "I think I should leave," he said under his breath. "I'll see you all later."

"Take care of yourself, Captain," Agnes called as he swung onto Raven.

Esther watched him ride away and groaned as Agnes appeared at her side with water and bandages.

"I also found your belongings," the nurse said. She dropped Esther's bullet into David's old haversack, ignoring the disgusted look Esther gave her. "Once I get your arm wrapped up, I'm going to set up the tent right over top of you. We wouldn't want to disobey Captain Armstrong and let you up, now, would we?"

"I'll disobey him in a heartbeat as soon as I need to use the privy," Esther whispered fiercely, and Agnes giggled again.

"He's been quite a friend to you," she said, ripping a rag in two. "Bringing you here and all when there is a battle going on. I think you're still ahead of him, though. You probably saved his life, you know."

Esther flinched as the young woman began washing the gash in her arm. "Try to relax," Agnes told her. "You'll mend faster if you take some time to only worry about yourself. You can't help anyone else now, but you'll be able to soon if you concentrate on getting better." She finished dressing the wound. "Now get some rest."

For the remainder of that day and the next, musket and cannon fire roared in the near distance. Resting was hard to do, and no matter what Agnes had told her, Esther constantly worried about Daniel. She tossed on the narrow cot, so miserable she wanted to cry. That afternoon she overheard Agnes tell one of the wounded men that it was July third.

David's birthday is the fifth, she thought. *He would have turned twenty-one this year.*

The cannons stopped booming, and before long it started raining. The raindrops pelting down on the tent added to her frustration. Remembering the peace she had been given the night she dreamed her father came home, she prayed again.

"God," she whispered, "I don't know why you took my family away, but I'm tired of trying to understand. I just know I need you here with me. Please, give me your peace. And keep Dad safe down there in that Confederate prison."

The last sentence was an afterthought, but it remained on her mind. He had said in his letter that he would pray for her every day.

Pray for me extra hard today, Daddy, she thought, and finally fell asleep.

"Wake up, Esther." Agnes' gentle voice was insistent. "Your captain is here to see you."

Esther rubbed her eyes and sat up. Daniel stood behind Agnes.

"You're alive!" she exclaimed, feeling limp with relief.

He gave her a half-grin and sat in the chair Agnes brought from the corner of the tent. "How are you feeling by now?" he asked, glancing at her arm.

"Much better." She smiled. "To be honest, I've been quite cranky the last couple days. Agnes and Florence didn't know what to do with me. But I promise I will behave according to my age from now on."

"You will?" Daniel grinned, cocking an eyebrow at her.

Esther shifted and tucked a strand of hair behind her ear. "Who won the battle?"

He frowned. "I'm not sure. The Confederates retreated, so I guess we did, but it didn't feel like it. Most of my company—and from what I've heard, most of my entire brigade—was either killed or wounded. Our army is pulling out to follow the Rebels, so I can't stay long, but I wanted to check on you."

He grimaced. "I finally met Miss Florence Ryan. She is one fierce old nurse. She wouldn't let me inside the tent until Miss Whitaker arrived and told her I was allowed to see you."

Esther smiled, picturing Florence barricading the front of the tent, her arms crossed. "That doesn't surprise me."

Daniel grinned. "And Miss Whitaker says you've been very obedient to my previous orders."

With her left hand, Esther saluted smartly. "Yes, sir, Captain Armstrong."

Daniel rolled his eyes. "Don't 'sir' me," he groaned. "I get enough of that from new recruits and junior officers who want to make a good impression."

She laughed, and Daniel stood up. "If there's ever anything I can do for you, don't hesitate to write me. Use the same address you used when you wrote David."

Esther nodded. She still knew the address by heart, but it seemed so long since she'd written David. "All right. I will."

He took her good hand in both of his for a moment. "Good-bye," he said. "Take care of yourself."

"I will," she said again. "Good-bye."

Daniel plunked his hat onto his head and returned the chair to the corner.

Then he was gone.

25. Healing and Helping

Esther's arm healed quickly. After three more days, she was out of bed and helping with the wounded, though Agnes didn't allow her to carry anything heavy for several weeks. Close to the end of July, when Esther was able to carry her full share of the work, she found out that the Second Corps hospital unit was planning to rejoin their corps soon. They would transfer their remaining patients to Camp Letterman, a collection of tents northeast of Gettysburg.

Florence and Agnes were planning to accompany the patients to the new hospital and continue nursing the wounded. Esther finally decided to go with Florence and Agnes because she didn't want to go home yet.

During her week of indecision, she wrote a short letter to Daniel, explaining the situation and asking his opinion. Then she nearly forgot about it, figuring he wouldn't receive it any-time soon.

At the beginning of August, all the patients except six had been moved to Camp Letterman and most of the tents were packed up. The Second Corps field hospital planned to leave the next day to rejoin their unit.

As Esther fetched water from Rock Creek to wash the supper dishes, she heard a familiar voice behind her.

"Esther! Miss Whitaker told me I would find you here."

She turned, dropping the bucket. "Daniel!"

He grinned at her. "I received your letter and was delighted at the chance to order around a willing person. Now, I think—"

"You're rushing to conclusions, Captain." Esther smiled as she tried to imitate the drawl he'd used on Agnes when they first met her. "You're too late. I've decided to go to Camp Letterman with Agnes and Florence."

He raised his eyebrows and laughed. "I'm glad you're staying with them. How are you, Esther? You look well. "

"Agnes took very good care of me. I'm glad you made sure I got back to her in one piece."

Daniel grunted. "It was the least I could do. I will never for-get how you saved my life." He took her hand and squeezed it. "Thank you, Little Birdie."

Esther drew in a sharp breath, jerking her hand away and staring at him. "That was the last thing David said to me," she whispered.

The pain of losing him swept over her—a pain so strong it squeezed her insides and left her fighting for breath. Daniel stepped toward her, and she said, "I'm all right. I just miss him." She bit her lip. "So badly."

She hardly realized she was crying until sobs shook her, and all the hurt, loneliness, and confusion of the past year came pour-ing out. She wasn't sure how long she cried, but the deep pain she'd felt since David's death drained away, leaving a dull ache.

Taking a long, shuddery breath, Esther realized Daniel's arm was around her shoulders. She turned around to glance up at him, and he reached into one pocket and then the other, pulling out a handkerchief.

"Thank you," she croaked, taking it and blowing her nose.

"I shouldn't have used that nickname, Esther," he said quietly, his eyes on the ground. "I'm sorry. Are you going to be all right?"

Rock Creek gurgled beside them, and Esther's heart felt lighter than it had for a long time. "Please don't apologize, Daniel." She took a deep breath and looked away. "I haven't cried since David died. I couldn't, somehow. But what you said—it hurt so much that I finally did."

She gave him a shaky smile. "And it helped. Thank you."

Daniel blinked, and his shoulders relaxed. He walked to the bucket she had dropped earlier and filled it. Esther knelt beside the creek, splashing cold water over her face, and then they walked back toward the dismantled camp.

"I have to return to my men," Daniel said slowly, turning to face her not far from where Raven was tied to a tree. "I am convinced by now that you can take care of yourself, but if there is anything I can do for you, all you have to do is ask."

Esther nodded. "Thank you, for everything."

He smiled at her. "You are most welcome. Good-bye."

"Good-bye." She wished he didn't have to leave. So many soldiers never returned home alive, and she was afraid to lose him too.

"Please don't die," she said quietly.

Daniel stopped abruptly and turned back to her. "What did you say?"

She looked down, half-embarrassed she'd spoken her thoughts.

"Esther?" He waited.

"I said please don't die," she repeated, lifting her head to meet his gaze. Her voice caught on the last word, and she looked down again, mortified.

Why can't I stop being so emotional? she wondered, eyeing her shoes.

"Esther, I am not on my way to a battle." His voice sounded strange.

"I know."

For a moment there was complete silence. Behind her back, Esther scrunched the handkerchief around her sweaty palms, her eyes burning with tears. Exhausted by reliving David's death and crying for so long, she suddenly wanted to be alone. She could feel Daniel staring at her, and she felt like squirming.

He moved toward her, and she looked up. But before she could meet his eyes, he spun on his heel and walked to his horse. She stared after him, wondering what he was thinking.

Daniel mounted Raven and rode away. When Esther turned to go back to the tents, she almost tripped over the bucket of water at her feet.

One night after Daniel's visit, Esther told Agnes all about David—how he had joined the army, been wounded at the second battle of Bull Run, and died in their home after they brought him back from Virginia. Agnes was a good listener, hugging Esther when she cried.

Caring for the wounded men at Camp Letterman kept Esther busy, and she was delighted every time a soldier recovered enough to leave. Near the end of November, she wrote two letters.

Dear Daniel,

I saw President Abraham Lincoln! I had to tell someone, so I'm writing you and the Washburns. I don't know about you, but I'm sure the Washburns will be impressed.

President Lincoln came to Gettysburg on November nineteenth and gave a speech, dedicating part of the battlefield as a cemetery for the soldiers who died there. Agnes, Florence, and I all went to hear him. There were so many other people there that we couldn't get very close, and I couldn't hear all of his speech, but I did see him! He looked tired and sad, as if he is responsible for more than his share of this world's troubles.

That was only a few days before Camp Letterman shut down. When there were no longer any wounded men to care for, I found out something my dear friends had not told me in the three months I've been with them.

Can you believe that Florence is actually Agnes's aunt? I never would have thought it! And before they volunteered as nurses, they lived with Agnes's mother in Gettysburg! Her name is Edith, and she has a little yellow house on the east end of town.

The day before the last two soldiers left Camp Letterman, Florence told Agnes to go talk to her mother before rushing off to join up with the army again. I guess the only reason Agnes's mother let her volunteer was because Florence agreed to go with her. But that was over a year ago, and Florence wanted to go home now. So we went to Edith's little yellow house in Gettysburg, and she persuaded us to stay with her and help her take care of Riley.

Riley is Agnes's nephew. He is almost a year and a half and the most adorable baby I have ever met, with big brown eyes and dimples. His father, Agnes's brother, is in the army, and his mother was killed during the fighting here this summer. The poor little fellow has had a hard life, but with four women to look after him now, he probably has more attention than is good for him.

We have all helped Edith and the neighbors clean up from the battle, and I have started working at a milliner's shop three days a week. The milliner, Charlotte, lost her assistant to typhoid after the battle, along with several other townspeople who were also helping the wounded. Charlotte has seven young children to care for, so I've been helping her run the store. I don't know how long I'll stay here in Gettysburg, but I love my adopted family, and I'm enjoying my work.

How are you faring? And our army? I heard about the siege of Vicksburg, Mississippi, and the battle of Chickamauga in Georgia. Both those places sound very far away. How much longer will this war go on?

Signing her name, Esther slid Daniel's letter into an envelope, quickly addressing it and the similar letter she'd written to the Washburns.

She blotted her ink and laid her pen across the inkwell. She could hear Riley crying downstairs and shook her head. Agnes had gone to the neighbors with Florence after giving Esther some stationery, so Edith was alone with the baby.

Hurrying downstairs, she found Edith walking back and forth in the parlor, holding Riley as he squirmed and screamed.

Esther held out her hands. "Shall I take him?"

Edith handed him over, brushing back her gray hair with a sigh. "Please do. He's cutting more teeth, and I don't know how to distract him anymore."

She sank down on the sofa, and Esther took Riley to the kitchen, scolding him in a playful voice. "Riley, how can you worry your poor grandmother like that?"

Riley stared at her, stuffing his fist into his mouth. His jerky sobs quieted a little.

Esther took him to the washbasin and set him on the edge. She poured water from the pitcher over his bare toes, and he giggled, showing his dimples through the tears on his cheeks.

Esther smiled at him. "I thought you might like that."

She wet her fingers and flicked them at his face. He sucked in a quick breath, jerking back and blinking his eyes before deciding he liked it.

"Gin," he gurgled. "Gin."

"Again?" Esther repeated, grinning.

She flicked her fingers at him again, and he laughed. She poured more water over his legs, and he patted them, sucking on his lip.

26. Triangle

"Charlotte reminded me that tomorrow is the day President Lincoln chose as a day of thanksgiving," Esther said one evening as she sat beside the parlor hearth darning socks.

Agnes looked up, her spinning wheel slowing. "Is it really?"

"Yes. He said the last Thursday in November." Esther pulled the finished sock off her darning egg and slid another one on, sighing at the size of the hole in the heel.

Agnes stopped spinning, her brown eyes lighting up. "We must celebrate it, then! I will ask Mama if I can kill a chicken, and you can ask Florence if she will use the sugar and spices she's been hoarding to make a pie. We'll set the table with our red tablecloth and Grandmama's china—"

"Why must I ask Florence?" Esther wanted to know, glancing through the kitchen doorway to where Florence was giving Riley his bath. "Are you afraid she'll refuse you?"

"No." Agnes began spinning again. "But I don't want to hear her lecture on the importance of being sober and solemn as we observe this day of thanksgiving. I think being thankful means being joyful, not solemn."

Esther grinned. "So you want me to hear the lecture."

"She won't give you a lecture, because you're sober enough to please her." Agnes's eyes twinkled. "But she's been encouraging me to be more demure ever since I was five, when I slapped the minister's son for kissing me and then ran home crying."

They both laughed.

After breakfast the next morning, Agnes killed and plucked a large rooster, and Esther helped her mince some beef suet, pieces of bread, parsley, sweet marjoram, lemon thyme, and onion. They added two eggs to the mixture and stuffed it into the chicken before sliding it into the oven.

"Something smells good!" Edith came into the kitchen as they finished, Riley on her hip. "Florence told me she is going to make pumpkin pie, and I see you two have prepared the chicken. Shall I make sweet potato pudding?"

Esther wiped her hands on her apron and looked at Agnes.

"Yes, do." Agnes took Riley from her mother and handed him to Esther. "Esther can look after Riley while I set the table."

Esther wrinkled her nose and went to change Riley's diaper.

They all feasted that night, and Esther felt very thankful for the acceptance she had found in Gettysburg.

One day late the next July, Esther escaped the heat of Edith's house and walked to Cemetery Ridge. She found some daisies growing among the shell-torn trees littering the hillside and picked some, suddenly wishing she could put them on her mother's grave.

It was a long time before she was ready to walk back to Gettysburg. As she came in sight of Edith's little yellow house, she noticed a brown horse tied to the wooden fence beside the road.

The horse twisted to look at her, swiveling its ears back and forth as she strolled up the road. When she turned through the gap in the fence, it whinnied.

Esther glanced behind her and then whirled, staring at the white patch on the horse's chest. "Triangle?" she gasped, dropping her daisies.

Snuffling, the horse threw its head up and down.

"Is it really you?" Esther stepped closer and touched the mare's muzzle, staring into her liquid brown eyes.

Esther threw her arms around the horse's neck. "Triangle!" She stepped back. "Where did you come from?"

Triangle whiffled through her nose and nudged Esther's shoulder.

"Stop it," Esther laughed. "Maybe Agnes knows." She headed for the house.

Behind her, the horse whinnied softly and tugged at the rope holding her to the fence.

"I'll be back in a minute," Esther called over her shoulder. "Stay there."

Triangle snorted.

Esther pushed open the door of the little house. "Agnes?" she called. "Do you know who tied that horse to the fence?"

Agnes came out of the kitchen. "What horse?"

Esther pointed out the window. "That horse. Triangle."

"So it is the right one." Agnes smiled. "He was hoping it was."

Esther frowned at her. "Agnes Whitaker, tell me what is going on."

Agnes smiled again. "Your friend, Captain Armstrong, stopped by."

"Daniel came on Triangle? Where is he?" Esther looked past Agnes eagerly.

"He isn't here anymore. He came right after you left and was terribly disappointed he missed you."

"So am I." Esther threw her bonnet on a chair and glanced out the window again. "Why is Triangle still here?"

"She belongs to you now." Agnes's smile crinkled the corners of her eyes. She took a paper from the table and held it out.

Esther took the note, scanning the words that were scrawled across its surface.

Riley is as adorable as you said, Esther. He couldn't stop saying your name the whole time I was here. I am sorry I missed you, but I cannot stay any longer. Miss Whitaker can explain about the horse. You have lost so much that I wanted you to have something back. Whether it is Triangle or not, I want you to keep her. Until we meet again, I remain your friend, Daniel Armstrong.

"Essa!" Riley crowed, toddling in.

Esther put the paper down and picked him up, kissing his forehead.

"Riley," she crooned against his cheek, "did you like Daniel? He brought my brother's horse back for me. See her out there by the fence? I'll take you on a ride sometime, all right?"

"If you ask me," Agnes said, coming to stand by them at the window, "that captain must have done a lot of sweet talking to whoever gave him permission to bring your horse back."

Esther glanced at her. "You're probably right. Where did he find her?"

Agnes shrugged. "He didn't tell me. He only said that he thought it was your brother's horse."

Esther smiled. "I'm so happy she's still alive."

Three days later Esther took Riley out behind the house to where she had tied her horse. "Do you want to ride Triangle, Riley?" she asked him, stroking the horse's neck.

Riley stared up at the horse and then turned his big, brown eyes on her. "Wide?" he repeated, the corners of his mouth turning up.

Esther nodded. "Yes, ride. Agnes?" she called, turning to where Agnes was hoeing in the garden. "Will you hand Riley up to me after I've mounted?"

Agnes put down her hoe and came toward them, frowning a bit. "Are you sure it's safe to take him for a ride without a saddle, Esther?"

Esther shrugged. "We'll just walk. She won't bolt with us, if that is what you're thinking."

Agnes still looked doubtful, but she held Riley as Esther tied the loose end of the rope to Triangle's halter to form reins. Tugging the horse over to the fence, Esther climbed onto Triangle's back and reached down for Riley, settling him in front of her.

"Be careful, Esther," Agnes cautioned. "If anything happens and Mama finds out I didn't stop you—"

"Relax, Agnes," Esther laughed. "Nothing will happen, and if it does, I will take full responsibility."

"All right." Agnes smiled. "Have fun, Riley."

Riley waved at Agnes as Esther urged Triangle out to the road. "Let's go out of town, Riley. Hang on."

"Essa?" Riley patted Triangle's neck, looking up at her questioningly.

"Triangle," Esther said, smiling at him. "Can you say that? Triangle?"

Riley stared at the horse's ears ahead of him for a moment. "Tangle," he announced proudly. "Wide Tangle."

Esther laughed. "You are so smart, Riley!"

He grinned, kicking his legs.

Esther rode to where Camp Letterman had been before turning Triangle back. As they stopped in front of the little yellow house, Edith came out and grabbed Triangle's halter.

"Esther, we just heard!" she said breathlessly. "Confederate soldiers raided and burned Chambersburg!"

Esther gasped. "Chambersburg! That's not very far away, is it?"

Edith shook her head, one hand fluttering up to pat down her lace collar. "Only about twenty-five miles." Her eyes softened. "Those poor people."

"Are the Confederates still here in Pennsylvania?" Esther asked.

Riley grunted, shifting about in front of her.

"No. I think some of our soldiers helped them decide to leave." Edith stepped closer, staring up at Riley. "I don't remember giving you permission to put my little boy up on that horse."

Esther grinned. "Neither do I. But you may have him now. I think he needs a clean diaper."

Edith rolled her eyes and sighed, pulling Riley down and carrying him gingerly to the house.

Esther tied Triangle at the fence in the back and went over to help Agnes pick lettuce. "Agnes, I want to go to Chambersburg," she said, breaking off several green leaves.

"The messenger said it was evacuated before it was burned, but there are probably still people who were hurt." Agnes glanced at her. "If that is what you mean."

Esther nodded. "I'm happy to have Triangle back, but there isn't a good place here to keep her. And Charlotte said her cousin is moving here next week to help with the store. If no one at Chambersburg needs help, I will go on home to Kirksville."

Agnes sighed. "I almost wish I could come with you, Esther. To Chambersburg, that is. I've a hankering to be a nurse again. But I should stay and help take care of Riley. I'll miss you."

Esther dropped the lettuce leaves into Agnes' wicker basket and hugged her. "Oh, Agnes, you know I'll miss you too. You've been such a good friend. More like a sister, really."

Agnes sniffled. "Have I been a better friend than that captain?"

Esther smacked her arm. "Stop it, Agnes. That's not fair to either of you."

Agnes giggled.

When Esther told Edith and Florence she was leaving, Edith cried, and Florence frowned, but they understood. Esther packed her things into her haversack and went up the street to say goodbye to Charlotte. Edith made fried chicken for supper that night, and Esther gave Riley his bath, tucking him into bed for the last time.

In the morning after an early breakfast, Esther slung her haversack over her shoulder and led Triangle out to the road, creating makeshift reins again with the end of the rope. Agnes, Florence, and Edith hugged her good-bye, and Agnes held Triangle's halter while Esther hugged Riley. Edith had woken him only minutes ago, and he was still blinking sleepily, a pattern of lines pressed into his cheek from the blanket.

Esther kissed him, squeezing his warm little body. "Goodbye, Riley," she whispered, her throat tight. "Be a good boy for your grandma and Aunt Agnes."

She handed him back to Edith and mounted Triangle, taking the bedroll Florence held up. Riley stretched out his arms.

"Wide Tangle gin?" he said hopefully.

Esther shook her head, nudging Triangle. "Not this time, Riley. I'm sorry. Good-bye, all of you."

"Good-bye," they chorused, and Riley squirmed in Edith's grasp. "Essa!" he shouted. "Essa!"

Esther bit her lip and guided Triangle up the street, tears pushing at her eyes. When she reached the milliner's store, Charlotte called out a good-bye from the porch, and Esther turned to look behind her, hearing Riley's shouts turn to wails. She could still see Edith, Florence, and Agnes waving at her from in front of the little yellow house.

Esther rode west on the Chambersburg Pike all morning. When the sun told her it was noon, she ate the sandwich Edith had sent along. Not long afterward, she reached Chambersburg.

Many of the buildings had been burned, but there were still parts of the town that were standing. Catching sight of three tents that promised to be a field hospital, she pulled Triangle up beside them and dismounted. Her sore legs almost buckled when her feet hit the ground. *It's been too long since I rode,* she thought, grimacing.

She undid one end of the rope from Triangle's halter and looked around, wondering where to tie her horse. Two men came out of the alley between two half-burned houses nearby.

"Good day," she called to them, hoping they could help her. She gave them a smile as they approached, but it faded when she saw their expressions.

They stopped a few steps away, the one with curly hair leering at her. "Good day," the other said, his voice not unfriendly.

"Never mind the pleasantries," the curly-haired one snapped. "You, girl," he added. "Hand over that horse."

Esther gripped Triangle's rope tighter. "Don't be ridiculous. She's mine." She tried to make her voice firm and strong, but it didn't work.

The curly-haired man chuckled derisively. "Who's being ridiculous?" he sneered. "The way I see it, it's one girl against two men."

He took a step forward, and Esther took one back, pulling Triangle's rope. The mare circled, confronting the ruffians with her hindquarters.

Esther looked around desperately. The flap of one of the tents was tied back, and she could see several people inside. "Help!" she shouted.

Two soldiers emerged and walked toward her. The older one was an officer and had a revolver strapped to his belt. He glanced at Esther.

"Are these men bothering you?" he asked.

"Of course not, officer," the curly-haired man said, eyeing the gun.

"Liar!" Esther exclaimed, glaring at the would-be thieves. "They are trying to steal my horse. I want them to go away and leave me *alone*." She jerked her arm back in a resentful motion.

The movement pulled Triangle's head down and snapped the end of the rope up so that it hit her belly. She reared and whinnied, pawing the air with her forelegs.

The slack in the rope slipped through Esther's fingers, and she realized she had accidentally given Triangle David's cues to rear. The curly-haired man gaped, but the other one jerked his arm, pulling him back to the alley.

Esther smiled, amazed that the horse had responded. Triangle had been with the army for over a year, and it had been even longer since David had been with her.

Shortening the rope, Esther tugged on it. "Easy, girl," she soothed. "Settle down now."

Triangle came down on all fours again, and Esther rubbed the mare's muzzle. "What a good girl," she murmured.

"Why did your horse do that?" the younger soldier quavered. "Is it vicious?"

Esther laughed. "No. It's an old trick my brother taught her," she explained.

The officer touched his fingers to his cap. "Are you quite all right, then, miss?"

Esther nodded. "Yes, thank you. But if it isn't too much trouble, could I ask you to find a safe place for my mare while I am helping with the wounded?"

"Certainly," the officer said. "I can tie her with my regiment's horses. They are always guarded, and you can come fetch her whenever you need to. We are camped just beyond that clump of trees." He pointed.

Esther handed him Triangle's rope. "Thank you so much," she said, flashing both of them a smile. She patted the mare's neck and watched as the officer led her away.

Esther stowed her haversack and bedroll by the nearest tent before going in and looking around. Most of the cots held civilians, but there were also some soldiers who had burns, probably from putting out fires in the town. They all looked miserable.

After Esther hunted up a bucket, dipper, and a nearby well, she carried water up and down the rows of cots, giving everyone a drink. Around the middle of the afternoon, she stepped out of the last tent and sat down in its shade. Her arm was sore from hauling the heavy bucket, and she was hungry.

Taking a deep breath, she stood back up and went into the first tent, where a doctor was treating the wounded. She told him she was a volunteer nurse and offered to help. He didn't seem very pleased, but he put her to work tearing bandages, fetching water, and dressing minor wounds.

At suppertime several ladies from town brought food for the wounded. Esther helped distribute bowls of soup to the patients in all three tents before she ate her own supper. It was dark when she crawled into her bedroll at the edge of one tent. The ground was hard, but she fell asleep instantly.

In the morning she helped distribute food and water again before heading to a big brick building with her bucket and dipper. She had seen people carrying stretchers and food in and out of it the day before.

There were two large rooms on the ground floor filled with cots and a small room off to the side that was being used for a kitchen. She had almost finished giving the men in the first row of cots a drink when someone called out behind her.

"Say, miss, can I have some of that water?"

Esther's heart stopped. She knew that voice!

27. Daniel's Only Chance

She spun around. "Peter Washburn!" she exclaimed, looking at the disheveled young man lying opposite her.

He stared back. "Esther? Esther *Sullivan*? What are you doing here?"

"What are *you* doing here?" Esther shot back. "You're supposed to be home with your family." Then she narrowed her eyes. "You ran off to join the army, didn't you?"

He squirmed. "A week ago when I turned eighteen."

Esther nodded. "And you only made it to Chambersburg before the raid happened and you got hurt."

She set her bucket on the floor and knelt beside his bed. His hair was singed, and the side of his face was burned. "Why are you here?" she asked. "What's wrong with you?"

Peter grimaced. "My leg." He propped himself up on one elbow and pulled the sheet away until she could see that his right leg lay at a crooked angle.

"I helped rescue some children from a burning house a couple days ago, and a beam fell on it. There aren't enough doctors to go around, so it hasn't been set yet."

He fell back, making a sound somewhere between a grunt and a moan. Esther gave him a drink, and he sighed, smacking his lips.

"That fellow beside me needs a doctor worse than I do." Peter motioned over her head to the bed beside his. "I think he's calling for his mother, or maybe his sweetheart or sister. I don't think he's old enough to have a daughter. Well, he could be, I guess. He keeps moaning and mumbling and saying, 'Please don't die.' Maybe he tried to save someone's life and he's afraid they didn't make it."

Esther twisted around. The uniformed man on the next bed was facing the other way, and she grabbed his shoulder, rolling him over.

"Daniel!" she gasped.

His eyes were closed, and his arms and legs twitched.

Peter stopped in mid-sentence and raised himself up on one elbow again. "You know him?" he asked in surprise.

Esther couldn't take her eyes from Daniel's face. He looked so sick. She placed her hand on his forehead and jerked it back. His skin was hot and dry.

"He was David's captain," she said softly. "He came with David once during their Christmas break and stayed overnight. That was the first time I saw him."

"You've seen him since?" Peter wanted to know. "You mean, while you were a nurse in the army?"

"Hush, Peter," Esther said. "I'll tell you later. Do you know what is wrong with him? Were you here when he was brought in?"

"No, I wasn't here, but I do know what is wrong with him." Peter flopped back, rubbing his arm. "The fellow in the bed on the other side of him—no, he isn't there anymore," he added. "That's a different fellow now. But the other one was well enough that he went home this morning, and he told me what was wrong with—what's your friend's name?—before he left."

"Daniel," Esther said.

Peter rambled on. "Because, although he was already delirious when they brought him in—Daniel was delirious, I mean, not the fellow that told me—two of his men brought him in and they told the fellow what had happened, and then he told me."

"Never mind how you heard," Esther grumbled. "Just tell me what is wrong with him."

Peter nodded. "He and his men came right as the raiders were leaving, and one of them shot him in his leg. It was a long-range shot, so it didn't rip up his leg that much, and he kept walking on it, helping put out the fires. It has been over four days since he was shot, and the bullet is still in there."

Over four days? Esther's heart sank. *No wonder his fever is so bad.* She dipped the last of the water from the bucket and carefully poured it into Daniel's mouth.

"Peter, I'm going to fetch a doctor to set your leg and take out Daniel's bullet," she announced, heading out of the room.

When she reached the first of the three tents, she picked up her haversack and bedroll. "Sir," she said, marching up to the doctor, "there are two soldiers in that brick building who need medical assistance. Will you come over briefly and take care of their wounds? Please?"

"I'm sure there are hundreds of patients in that brick building who need medical assistance," the doctor huffed. He scrunched his bushy eyebrows together. "Wait until I'm finished with this fellow, and then I'll come with you."

Esther sighed. He hadn't even started unwrapping the wound yet! But she said, "Thank you, sir," and waited until he was done.

After gathering up a few of his medical tools, he followed her to the brick building. It did not take him long to set Peter's leg and secure it in a splint, but when he looked at Daniel, he shook his head.

"This one is too far gone," he said. "I can't waste my time on him. There are too many others who need my help."

Esther flinched. *Too far gone? Waste of time?* "Please, doctor," she begged, "if you take out his bullet, I will clean and wrap the wound."

The doctor shook his head again. "It isn't worth my time," he repeated. "It's doubtful he'll pull through this fever. I'm sorry."

Esther crossed her arms as she watched him leave. "If that isn't the meanest, most despicable—" She pressed her lips together and groaned.

"What are you...talking about?" Peter's voice was unsteady. The pain of having his leg set had made him groggy.

Well, I can't depend on that doctor, Esther thought, setting her jaw.

She pulled Daniel's trousers up to his knees and found the place in the calf of his left leg where the bullet had gone in. The skin was starting to close over it, but the wound was infected. It would have to be reopened and the bullet removed for it to heal properly.

Her stomach twisted. He would probably lose his life if the infection wasn't taken care of. She took David's knife from her haversack and tested the blade.

"What are you doing with that knife?" Peter asked.

"I have to take out his bullet," she answered, walking away as he babbled about her not being a doctor.

She went to the room being used as a kitchen, and the two ladies there gave her a pot to boil some water. She didn't tell them why she was sterilizing the knife, suddenly unsure of herself.

But who else would help Daniel? She was his only chance.

When the knife was ready, she carried it and the rags she had collected to Daniel's bed. *Thank you, God,* she thought fervently, seeing that Peter was asleep. He would have hung over her arm, questioning and advising her on every move.

Esther bit her lip and forced herself to make the first cut into Daniel's leg. He moaned, and she worked faster, determined to remove the bullet and infection.

Daniel didn't move much, and Peter didn't wake up. Esther's breathing slowed to normal, and she sighed with relief when she held up the bullet at last. She washed the wound well and bandaged his leg, praying God would give him the strength to heal.

The rest of the day, she answered and evaded Peter's questions and took care of Daniel. He was burning with fever, and she sat beside him most of the afternoon, sponging his face, arms, and hands with cool water.

For the first two days after she had removed his bullet, he remained delirious, mumbling, "Please don't die," as he tossed and turned.

Esther slept between Daniel's and Peter's cots, and both nights she fell asleep on her knees, begging God to heal Daniel. She had never felt more desperate.

"You saved his life once before, God, when that bullet hit me instead of him," she whispered. "Please give him one more chance."

On the morning of the third day, he was breathing easier when she changed his bandage. She put her hand on his forehead and found that it was cool and moist.

"Peter, look!" she exclaimed, not caring that she was waking him up. He could sleep any time he wanted to.

"Look at what?" he grumped sleepily.

"Daniel's fever broke!" Esther hugged herself and felt like crying. She gave a little twirl in the narrow space between the cots and bumped into Peter's.

He cried out at the jolt to his leg. "Esther, please," he whimpered, fully awake now. "Be a little more careful."

Esther bent over him, straightening his sheet. "I'm sorry, Peter," she whispered. "But isn't it exciting about Daniel?"

"I suppose," Peter agreed, turning his head away.

Esther hummed as she finished wrapping Daniel's leg. The doctor passed that afternoon, and he stopped to look at them, frowning.

"This is the broken leg I set," he said, pointing to Peter and then to Daniel. "Is this the fellow you wanted me to take a bullet out of?" he asked Esther.

"Yes. I took it out myself."

"Did you?" The doctor looked mildly surprised. "May I see it?"

Esther raised her eyebrows. "The bullet or the wound?"

The doctor huffed through his nose. "The wound, my dear girl, the wound. Do not be absurd."

Esther put down her knitting and unwrapped Daniel's bandage.

"I can hardly believe it!" the doctor exclaimed, examining Daniel's leg. "He must have a strong will to live. I'll come back and check on him again tomorrow. His fever has broken, so he should keep improving. Keep on doing whatever you're doing to him, because it's working."

For a moment Esther was speechless. "I will, Doctor," she replied at last, smiling. "Thank you."

The next morning she carried water around to all the patients who wanted a drink. Peter was asleep when she passed his bed, but when she looked at Daniel, he was staring at her.

"Esther?" His voice was incredibly weak. "What are you doing here?"

She knelt beside his bed, beaming so hard her face hurt. "I found you while I was helping with all the wounded. And you are finally awake! How do you feel?"

"Tired," he murmured, closing his eyes. "Tired and ridiculously weak."

She smiled and stood up. "That's because you haven't eaten for so long. I'll bring some food right away."

"Esther."

She glanced back.

He was looking at her, the corners of his mouth turning up in a faint smile. "I didn't die."

She squeezed his hand where it lay motionless on the sheet. "I'm so glad." She bit her lip. "I worried when you were delirious, but your fever broke, and the doctor says you will keep recovering."

"Thank you, Esther," Daniel whispered.

In the kitchen one of the ladies gave her some broth with vegetables and meat in it. She carried it to Daniel and saw that Peter was awake.

"Good morning, Peter," she greeted him brightly. "Have you introduced yourself to Daniel yet?"

Peter ran his hands through his hair and yawned a big, gaping yawn. "Who's talking about introductions?" he said. "I'm still waking up."

Esther laughed and sat down on the chair she had squished between the two cots. "Daniel, this is Peter Washburn, one of my neighbors, and Peter, this is Daniel Armstrong, David's captain. Say hello to each other for me."

Daniel obliged, but Peter did not.

"I will say hello later," he griped at Esther, "not when you tell me to. I don't feel like talking to anyone right now."

"Good!" Esther crowed. "Why didn't you say so sooner? I will give Daniel his breakfast, and you will not disturb me, even to ask for your own breakfast."

Peter grunted, frowning.

Daniel winked at Esther as he hungrily swallowed the soup she was spooning into his mouth. She grinned.

Over the next two weeks Daniel continued to improve, but his progress was so slow that Esther almost despaired. The doctor, who checked on him every few days, told her to be patient.

Esther kept helping the ladies who worked in the kitchen, and the doctor when she could. One day Peter finally persuaded her to sit and tell him everything that happened since she had left home.

After she finished her story, he had the nerve to ask Daniel if it was really as plain and boring as she made it out to be. Daniel just laughed.

One of the kitchen ladies lived on a farm outside town and offered to let Esther keep her horse there. When Esther returned after putting Triangle into their pasture, Daniel showed her the honorable discharge he had just received from the army.

"I was tired of fighting this war," he said, closing his eyes. "None of it makes sense anymore."

Esther sat down on the chair between the cots, still looking at the piece of paper. It was very much like the one David had received. "Daniel, whatever happened to Raven?" she asked. "Riding Triangle today reminded me of him."

"Raven was shot out from under me during the raid," Daniel said, biting his lip. "He survived all the battles we've been through only to be killed in my last encounter with the Rebels."

Esther looked up at him, stunned. "I'm so sorry."

Daniel sighed. "So am I."

28. A Suitable Arrangement

One afternoon, Esther sat between Daniel and Peter, knitting. The next day was her birthday, and thinking about it made her homesick.

"You look gloomy," Daniel observed.

She glanced up. "Oh. I didn't know you were awake." She looked back at her hands.

"You do now," he declared pertly.

Esther felt even lonelier. Stating the obvious had been David's specialty.

"Is something wrong, Esther?"

She shook her head. "Not really."

"Care to tell me what you were thinking about?"

She sighed. "It's nothing important, only that tomorrow is my birthday, and I want so badly to go home. I want to sleep in my own bed again and see the Washburns and Milksop and—" She blinked back tears.

"Tomorrow is your birthday?" Daniel repeated.

Peter turned his head in their direction. "You can see me, Esther. I am a Washburn."

"Hush, Peter," Daniel ordered.

Esther sniffed and wiped her nose with the back of her hand. "I'll be nineteen tomorrow, and here I am, crying, 'I want to go home,' like a child."

Peter snickered, but he didn't say anything.

"That's understandable, Esther," Daniel said. "You've been away a long time."

"Yes." Esther sat up straighter. "And I'm deciding right now to go home. When I went to see Triangle yesterday, I found a wagon for sale. I am going to buy it this afternoon and take both of you back to Kirksville. You can finish getting better there."

Daniel looked startled, and Peter actually gasped.

"But I ran away," he protested. "What if they don't want me back?"

"Don't be silly." Esther shook her head at him. "Your family will be tremendously glad to see you, and you know it."

"Esther?"

She turned to Daniel. "What?"

"What are you going to do with us when we get to Kirksville? Peter can go back to his family, but I don't want to impose on their hospitality, and I can't stay at your house. It wouldn't be proper."

Esther stared at him and then sighed. "You're right." She frowned. "But we can't stay here forever, either. Peter is getting too lazy, and—"

"I have a bum leg! What else can I do but lie here?"

"And we'll figure out where you'll stay when we get home, Daniel," Esther finished.

She stood up and put her nearly completed sock on her chair, bending over Peter. "There's nothing wrong with your hands," she said. "Maybe Priscilla could teach you to knit."

Esther straightened. "I'll be back after a while," she told them.

She still had some of her father's emergency money, and after she bought the wagon, she purchased food and supplies for the trip to Kirksville. The kitchen ladies gave her old blankets to soften the wagon bed for Daniel and Peter and packed them a basket of food.

Esther was tired when she rolled into her blanket that night, but it was a long time before she fell asleep. She couldn't stop thinking of leaving for home the next morning.

As Esther took the water bucket around for the last time before breakfast, everyone in the room suddenly chorused, "Happy Birthday, Miss Sullivan!"

She put down the bucket and covered her ears, but she laughed. "Whose idea was that?"

"Daniel's," Peter burst out, beaming as proudly as if it had been his idea.

"It's a small way of trying to say thank you, Esther," Daniel said. "You've helped everyone here."

Esther felt warm inside. "You're welcome, then," she replied, smiling around the room. "Thank you for thinking of me."

After breakfast, two men helped Daniel and Peter out to the wagon. The doctor followed Esther out of the brick building.

"Of all the nurses who've helped me, you were one of the best," he told her. "I could tell that you cared about the patients."

He cautioned her to keep Daniel's wound clean and not let Peter put weight on his leg for several more weeks. The kitchen ladies came out to wave them off, and Esther waved back.

"Good-bye," she called, pulling on Triangle's halter.

"Good-bye," they returned. "Be safe."

The trip to Kirksville took over a week. Esther walked beside Triangle the whole way, picking out the smoothest part of the road. Peter still became restless and grouchy, and Daniel grew weaker from the inevitable jostling.

Esther started to wonder if she had done the right thing in moving him before he was completely well. There was nothing she could change now, so she kept pushing on toward home, taking care of him as best she could and trying to be patient with Peter.

The trees were turning red and orange, signaling the beginning of autumn. Esther admired them briefly, feeling tired. She hardly thought of anything but finding the best place to spend the night and hoping Daniel would eat his share of what she cooked.

Esther stopped Triangle outside Kirksville so they could eat lunch, but Daniel was asleep and Peter wasn't hungry, so she grasped Triangle's halter and went on. They paused at Doctor Cunningham's house, and Esther asked his wife to tell her husband that there were two patients at the Washburns for him to check on.

Esther's heart beat faster as her house came into sight, and she thought it looked empty and lonely. They went past it to the Washburns' house, and Peter dragged himself to a sitting position, clinging to the side of the wagon as Esther tied Triangle to the hitching post.

She helped him out of the wagon and up the steps. From the sounds inside, the family was eating lunch.

Esther lifted her hand to knock on the door, and Peter drew back.

"Are you sure they will want to see me?" he whispered, sounding scared.

"Of course." Esther threw open the door, figuring no one would hear her if she knocked. "I've brought Peter home," she announced, pulling him inside with her.

Mrs. Washburn turned and said, "Esther?"

Mr. Washburn gasped, "Peter?" and sprang from his seat, hugging his son and rocking him back and forth.

Priscilla stood up and shook her finger at him. "Peter! You are a naughty boy!"

The other children crowded around until Mrs. Washburn intervened, hugging Esther and Peter and insisting they sit at the table and eat.

Esther had not forgotten about Daniel, and while she ate, she told the Washburns his story. "The only family he has left is an older brother in Ohio, and he's so far away and has lots of little children. I want to take care of Daniel until he's well enough to leave on his own, if he wants, but it wouldn't be proper to just take him to my house. What should I do?"

"Daniel can stay here, of course," Mr. Washburn said. "And so can you."

"Think of the noise, though." Priscilla wrinkled her nose at Nicolas and Jacob. "He'd never get any rest."

Peter groaned. "Neither will I."

Mr. and Mrs. Washburn looked at each other.

"What if," Mrs. Washburn suggested slowly, "Esther and Priscilla would care for Daniel and Peter at the Sullivan's house? There would be plenty of room, and I think it would be entirely proper."

Esther thought for a moment. "I can't think of anything better." She sighed and then smiled. "Daniel can have my parents' room, and Peter can sleep on the sofa. We girls can stay upstairs."

"I could have a room to myself!" Priscilla exclaimed, smiling at Esther.

Victoria slipped her head under her mother's arm and whispered something in her ear.

Mrs. Washburn looked at Esther. "Won't you get lonely, Esther, if Priscilla is in a different room?"

"Well," Esther said, catching the hint in Mrs. Washburn's voice, "not if you'd let Victoria stay with me. She could help me make breakfast too, since Priscilla doesn't like getting up early. Would you like that, Victoria?"

Victoria beamed, and Mrs. Washburn nodded, smiling at Esther.

"I think it's a great plan." Mr. Washburn clapped his hands together. "We'll bring supper over as often as Daniel can stand the noise."

"Thank you so much for your help!" Esther stood up. "I had no idea what to do."

"It will be easier this way," Mrs. Washburn said. "There will only be one house with wounded men lying around.

"Priscilla and Victoria, why don't you go pack up some clothes for yourselves, and Sarah, you pack some for Peter."

Mrs. Washburn bustled around, pulling baking supplies from the kitchen shelves and sending Nicolas and Jacob to the root cellar for vegetables.

Esther went out to help arrange everything in the wagon. Daniel was rubbing sleep from his eyes, and she told him their plan and asked him what he thought.

"Sounds great," he groaned. "Anything to get out of this wagon."

On the way over to her house, Esther asked Priscilla, "Is Lydia still working at the General Store in town?"

"No, she's married," Priscilla said. "Didn't Peter tell you?"

Esther shook her head, speechless.

"Oh." Priscilla thought a moment and then plunged on. "She didn't get married until after he ran away. Before that he was likely caught up with his own plans and didn't notice what was going on around here much. But he *did* know."

"Who did she marry?" Esther finally thought to ask.

"A soldier from town who lost his left arm at Antietam." Priscilla made a face. "He's a nice fellow, and I'm glad for her, but now she lives fully ten miles away, and we only get to see her on Sundays. I won't mind it so much, though, now that I get to live with you."

After fresh linens were spread on the beds in the Sullivan house, Mr. Washburn and Nicolas carried Daniel into Esther's parents' bedroom. Esther packed away all of David's things and let Priscilla stay in his old room.

The living room was Peter's domain. He slept sprawled across the sofa, and during the day, whenever he got a burst of energy or became restless, he would hobble about on a crutch that Nicolas had made for him. Since the crutch was not the proper height and Peter had to hunch over when he used it, the girls laughed at how ridiculous he looked.

Daniel ran a high fever for two days after they reached home, and though he wasn't delirious, Esther worried about him. Doctor Cunningham stopped by and said Peter had to wear his splint for another three weeks.

After examining Daniel, he tugged at his beard. "Keep sponging his face and arms, and try to make him eat. It's hard for his body to fight when he is so weak. I will stop in often to check on him. You've been doing a wonderful job, Esther."

Esther smiled. "Thank you, Doctor Cunningham. I'm glad you're nearby."

She fetched some money to pay him, but he refused to take more than half of it. "These boys were wounded while they were serving our country, and the least I can do is help them recover," he said.

Tears stung Esther's eyes at his generosity. "Thank you, Doctor," she said again.

After showing him out, she took a water pitcher upstairs, filling the one in Priscilla's room and then her own. Pulling out her odds-and-ends drawer, she looked down at her mother's necklace, the plaque of Triangle, *Highland Rose,* dozens of letters, and David's uniform. Lifting the plaque, she ran her eyes over it.

I forgot how good it was, she thought, running her fingers over the mark in the horse's belly where David's knife had slipped.

Closing the drawer, she set it up against the wall on top of the chest of drawers.

"It's like David's life," she murmured. "Beautiful, even though it was never finished." She closed her eyes for a moment. *David, I miss you.*

Unpacking her haversack, she found a bullet at the bottom. *I nearly forgot Agnes put it in here,* she thought, rolling the bullet between her fingers and dropping it into the drawer beside David's uniform.

Memories of her time with the army flooded her mind, and she closed her eyes again. "Thank you, God, for keeping me safe."

After Peter's three weeks were up and his splint came off, he and Esther took turns staying home with Daniel on Sundays while the others went to church.

Priscilla never took a turn since she didn't want to miss a chance to see Lydia. Peter complained, scolding her for her selfishness, but Esther didn't mind. Daniel was getting stronger, and on her Sunday mornings with him she read aloud from the Bible and they talked.

Once the twins bickered over who would drive Triangle to church, and Victoria admonished them to be good, since it was Sunday. After they left, Esther described it to Daniel, and they laughed so hard that tears squeezed from Esther's eyes.

"Daniel, what is your favorite color?" Esther asked later, after she'd finished reading the Bible aloud and was working on her knitting.

He grinned his lopsided grin. "Why? Are you going to knit me a scarf for Christmas?"

She sniffed. "I thought Victoria understood not to tell."

Daniel looked guilty. "She wasn't going to. I coaxed for a very long time before she gave me any hints."

Esther poked at him with a knitting needle.

"My favorite color is yellow," he said quickly, scooting away. "Like the goldenrod in the fall and the leaves when they change color. And orange, I guess. The leaves turn orange too."

"I am not knitting you a yellow scarf or an orange one," Esther said firmly. "Pick a different color."

"What are those purple flowers that always grow with goldenrod? Asters?"

"Purple is not much better than yellow, Daniel."

Daniel sighed. "I've always longed for a purple scarf, Esther," he said dramatically. "But maybe I should settle for brown."

Esther couldn't help but laugh. "I think brown would be the best choice."

"What is your favorite color?"

"Blue. The soft blue of the sky when the sun is coming up and the deep, intense blue of a cloudless sky on a hot summer day." Her voice faltered. "That was the color of David's eyes," she whispered. "Deep, intense blue."

She stopped knitting and stared at her fingers, picturing her brother's curly black hair and dimpled grin.

"Sitting here, the way I did with David—" Esther said slowly. "I can't help but think of when he died, and it hurts all over again."

She choked on the last words and started crying, covering her face with her hands as she fought to breathe past the ache in her heart.

"I'm sorry," she whispered after a moment, wiping her eyes.

"You don't have to apologize," Daniel said softly.

Another tear slid down Esther's cheek. "Thank you," she murmured, trying to swallow the lump in her throat.

Daniel chuckled a little later, his brown eyes lighting up.

Esther rubbed her nose and started knitting again. "Why are you laughing?"

He smiled, shaking his head. "I just remembered something that happened when David and I were training new recruits in the spring of sixty-two. He was teaching the men how to load and shoot their muzzle-loaders quickly and accurately. There were three fellows who took longer than everyone else to master the loading part. And once they had, they couldn't seem to hit the target, even though David made them practice for almost an hour.

"He told them, 'You fellows have to shoot better than that if you want to be in General Kearny's army!' He kept throwing that line at them, dancing around and encouraging them to do better."

Esther envisioned her brother, hair askew and red in the face, pleading with the new recruits to improve. She grinned, glancing at Daniel when he didn't continue.

"What were you grinning about?" he wanted to know.

She told him, and he laughed. "David was usually neat, but for some reason his trousers were wrinkly that morning, and his coat was only half-buttoned. I think he even had the buttons in the wrong holes, so he looked lopsided.

"And then General Kearny walked up. He had been reviewing the company next to ours, and when he heard David shouting his name, he came to see why.

"When David caught sight of the general, he told the recruits, 'Look, there is the general himself. If you really want to be in his army, show him what you can do!'

"The recruits all tried again, doing much better, and David headed for a tent to hide. But before he disappeared, the general called him back.

"'Lieutenant!' he said. 'I want to see you shoot.'"

"David has a very good aim," Esther interrupted, remembering her snowball fights with her brother. Her voice dropped. "*Had*, I mean."

Daniel glanced at her before continuing. "He impressed the general with his swiftness and accuracy when he shot. General Kearny told the recruits they should try to become like their lieutenant in everything except the way he dressed."

Esther laughed outright.

"David apologized for the way he looked and said it wouldn't happen again. It didn't, but he never quite got over his embarrassment."

Esther grinned. "Poor David. Let me tell you about something else he did a long time ago."

She settled back in her chair, her fingers steadily wrapping the yarn around her needles. "He was thirteen, so I was ten, Lydia was eleven, and the twins were nine. David and Peter had made a raft of logs and put it in our creek. They persuaded us girls to get on it and see if it would hold our weight. Tying it to a tree may have been the right thing to do, but when the raft drifted to the end of the rope, it stopped with a jerk, and we girls fell off.

"That was when I learned how to swim. I thought David meant for us to fall off, and I got so mad at him. As soon as I climbed out onto the bank, I went over and pushed him into the creek. I think I called him a wicked boy."

Daniel chuckled. "Esther!"

Esther grinned at him and continued her story. "Lydia and Priscilla shoved Peter in too, and we girls stood there on the bank, crying and scolding our brothers. After they got over being surprised, they started swimming around and having a good time. That made us even more mad. No one ever used the raft again. I think Dad took it apart and used it for firewood."

Daniel laughed again. "What an appropriate fate."

Esther smiled and stood up. "I'd better go check the roast I put in the oven this morning."

29. False Hope?

Nicolas brought Milksop back over to the Sullivans' barn a week after their return, but Esther insisted they keep Daisy.

"You've earned her by taking such good care of our animals whenever we've been gone," she told Mr. Washburn when he protested. "Besides, I don't need two cows. What would I do with all the milk?"

Twelve-year-old Jacob and seven-year-old Caleb Washburn stopped in to collect Victoria every morning on their way to school. Esther and Priscilla took turns packing her a lunch and helping her with her homework.

"It's not fair that I'm the only one around here who has to go to school and do homework," Victoria complained one evening. She was struggling to subtract the sums Priscilla had copied out for her, and she had been working on the same one for several minutes.

"You can go and live with your family again," Esther suggested. "Then you won't be the only one doing your homework every evening."

Victoria stared at her for a moment, chewing on her lower lip. Then she bent over her paper and began to rework the sum. "There," she announced triumphantly, holding up the paper. "Is this right?"

Esther squinted at the numbers. "Yes, it is. Well done."

Victoria grinned. "I don't want to go back and live with my family yet," she said. "So I guess I should stop complaining."

When Christmas came Esther helped Victoria hang their stockings on the mantel. She looked at the photographs of her family and thought back to previous Christmases. Last year she was with Agnes, Florence, Edith, and Riley in Gettysburg. The Christmas before that, right after David died, had been miserable. Her brother had been on leave the year before, and that was when she'd first met Daniel.

Was it really only four years ago that we were all together? she wondered. *It feels like forever since Mama was with us.*

Early Christmas morning Priscilla came over to Esther's room. "Wake up, you two," she whispered fiercely, sticking her head in the door. "If we don't go down soon, Peter will have already gone through our stockings."

"He better not have." Victoria sat up and slid out of bed. "Come on, Esther," she urged, pulling her dress over her head. "Get up and come down with us."

Esther groaned and rolled over. "I'm still tired. You two go ahead, and I'll come down later."

She closed her eyes and after a moment felt the quilt being jerked away.

"We're going to make you come down now," Priscilla said firmly, pulling her out of bed. "How can you still be tired?"

"You usually are this time of day, Priscilla," Esther pointed out grumpily. "Or is it night?"

Victoria tugged Esther's dress from a peg on the wall and thrust it at her. "Aren't you excited at all?"

Esther heaved a sigh as she dressed. "Of course I am, but I am still tired." She shook back her hair. "Since you made me get up, I'm going to beat you downstairs."

As they hurried down the stairs, her parents' bedroom door opened, and Daniel appeared, his brown hair tousled. "No more sleep tonight, I guess," he said, glancing up at them.

To Esther's surprise, Peter was still asleep on the living room sofa when she and Victoria came in. Daniel and Priscilla were taking down their bulging stockings, and Daniel began stirring up the fire.

Victoria tiptoed closer to the sofa. "Should we wake him?" she whispered.

Daniel grinned. "Let's pounce on him."

Victoria giggled. "All right. But don't hurt him."

She stretched out a finger to poke Peter's leg, and Daniel limped behind the sofa to grab the arm that was thrown over the back.

"On three," Daniel hissed. "One, two—"

Peter shifted and started rubbing his eyes. "The Rebels," he mumbled, sitting up. "They marched in here to capture me, shouting and—" He looked around as Daniel sighed and Victoria dropped her arm. "Oh, it's only you."

"It's Christmas morning, Peter," Victoria said, returning to the fireplace. "We're making sure everyone is awake to look in their stocking."

Esther unhooked Victoria's stocking and then her own. "Be glad you woke up yourself, Peter," she told him. "They dragged me out of bed."

Daniel laughed, but Peter only yawned, running his fingers through his hair. "What is your hurry?" he wanted to know. "I already looked in my stocking. Last night before I went to sleep. Thanks for the socks, Esther."

"For shame, Peter!" Priscilla frowned at him. "Couldn't you have waited? I hope you didn't look in ours too."

Peter grinned. "Does it matter if I did?"

Priscilla huffed and sat down on the hearth, emptying her stocking into her lap. "A pin cushion! Esther, did you make this for me?" She held up a green, heart-shaped pin cushion. "Now I don't have to use yours."

"No, I made it. With Esther's help." Victoria pulled a little wooden doll out of her stocking. "Who is this from?"

Daniel put down his crutch and sat beside her. "It's from me. Do you like it?"

Victoria nodded, beaming. "I'm going to name her Amanda. Margaret and I can play with her this afternoon when they all come over for Christmas dinner." She cradled the doll in one arm and hugged Daniel with the other. "Thank you!"

Daniel hugged her back, trying to keep his balance. "You're welcome, Precious. It was fun working on that while I was lying in bed for so long."

Esther carried her stocking to the sofa, motioning for Peter to move over. He sat up and watched her shake her stocking into her lap.

"That's what I made you," he said, pointing to the long wooden spoon that had been sticking out the top. "Priscilla and Victoria made the handkerchiefs with your initials on them. And Daniel bought you something so big it wouldn't fit in your stocking."

"Are you supposed to be telling me about it?" Esther glanced over at Daniel. "Daniel, is Peter saying things he shouldn't be?"

Daniel laughed. "I bought you some dress fabric, Esther. It's behind the sofa."

Esther retrieved the package and sat back down before tearing it open. "Daniel, it's beautiful!"

Priscilla came over to finger the blue, flowery cloth. "I thought you would like it."

Esther eyed Priscilla, smiling. "You must have helped him pick it out," she said. "Thank you both."

Victoria tugged on Daniel's arm. "Daniel, what's in your stocking?"

Daniel held up his bulging woolen stocking and shot Esther a significant glance before turning to Victoria. "A scarf," he announced.

Victoria gave a little gasp and looked over at Esther, her blue eyes wide.

Esther held back a laugh. "That's a reasonable guess," she said. "Why don't you look and see."

Daniel's eyes twinkled, and he reached into his stocking, pulling out a brown scarf.

Victoria gasped again. "I thought you wanted a yellow one!"

Daniel shook his head mournfully. "Esther refused to make a yellow one. Or a purple one."

Esther laughed, unable to hold it in any longer.

A week later she wrote Agnes a letter, telling her friend about finding Daniel and her neighbor Peter in Chambersburg and bringing them home with her.

> Peter's leg healed quickly, and although Daniel has not yet regained his strength, he is hobbling around with the help of a crutch.
>
> I'm sure you heard that Abraham Lincoln was re-elected in the November elections. If anyone wishes for this war to be over, I'm sure he does. Can you imagine being in charge of our divided country? Mrs. Washburn, Peter's mother, says that she knows how he feels in a very small way when her children fight over things. Mr. Washburn, my source of information, says that the South is slowly losing ground. I hope that means the war will end soon.
>
> Please kiss Riley for me, and give my best to your mother and Florence. I miss you all.
>
> Lovingly,
>
> Esther Sullivan

On January third, Daniel's twenty-fifth birthday, Dr. Cunningham stopped in and said that Daniel's leg was completely healed and could be used again, which Esther thought was amusing. He had already been walking around on it for the better part of a week.

Esther invited the Washburns over that evening to celebrate Daniel's birthday, and Mrs. Washburn brought a jar of peach preserves that she said she had been saving for just such a special occasion.

Ever since Esther started reading the Bible to Daniel on Sundays, he had been reading it on his own. One morning in February, after the Hampton Roads Peace Conference had failed to end the war, Esther set a bowl of oatmeal on the table as Daniel came out and sat at the table. He had fretted over the incompetence of the leaders in Washington for the last three months, but this morning he looked surprisingly peaceful.

"Daniel?" She waited until he looked at her. "What happened? You are different somehow."

He looked startled and then grinned almost shyly. "I gave my life to God last night, Esther, and I *do* feel different."

She studied him for a moment, loneliness stealing through her. "You look happier." Her voice softened. "I'm glad for you, Daniel."

"Esther, will you come button my dress?" Victoria called from the top of the stairs.

Esther went to help her, thinking of when her brother enlisted in God's army. Once again, she felt left out of something good.

After that, Daniel read a Bible chapter aloud every night while they sat in the living room, talking or working. The way he made the Bible interesting, even for Victoria, reminded Esther of her father and made her long to see him.

Once on his way home from town, Mr. Washburn stopped in to deliver a letter.

"Thank you," Esther called after him, closing the door on the cold. She ripped open the envelope. "It's from Agnes!"

She pulled a chair out from the dining room table and sank into it as she read her letter.

Dear Esther,

I was thrilled to receive your letter and learn what happened after you left us. I am especially overjoyed to hear that Captain Armstrong is alive and well and no doubt in paroxysms of delight over your nursing abilities.

Esther rolled her eyes at Agnes's familiar teasing.

Mama and Florence wish me to convey their fondest hopes that you are doing well, and this blotted spot of ink is Riley's attempt to write something—I'm not sure what. He is growing so fast, but he still misses you. Right now he's saying your name and asking for another wide on Tangle. Perhaps that is what he was trying to write.

Esther touched the black ink stain and sighed as she remembered Riley's brown eyes and dimples and how he loved to play in water.

Now for my news. Did Charlotte tell you that her cousin was a quiet but very intelligent young man with black hair and unfathomable green eyes? Justin Tanner has come calling on me almost every Thursday evening for the past five months, and last week he asked me to marry him! I had told him once how much I love butterflies, and he gave me a brooch with a black swallowtail on it when he proposed to me. I thought it so romantic.

Don't you dare laugh, Esther, as Florence did. If she ever had a romantic fancy, she doesn't seem to remember it.

Justin is such a good man, and I am in raptures. He has a wonderful way of listening to me, making me feel that everything I say is important to him. We are to be married in May as soon as he has finished building an addition onto Mama's house. You must come visit us all sometime, or perhaps I can come visit you. Do write and tell me how you are, for I miss you very much.

Your friend,

Agnes Whitaker, soon to be Tanner

Esther smiled over Agnes's signature, picturing her friend's bright eyes and frizzy golden hair. *I'm so happy for you, Agnes,* she thought.

The door burst open, and Daniel and Peter stomped in. "It is so cold out there," Peter exclaimed, shivering.

Esther glanced up. "Did you get the fence mended?"

"Yes. It took longer than I'd hoped." Daniel pulled off his gloves and rubbed his hands together, blowing on them. "But now Milksop will stay where she belongs and not go wandering back to the Washburns' pasture."

"She probably thinks that *is* where she belongs, as much as she's been over there." Esther held up Agnes's letter. "Daniel, look what Mr. Washburn brought."

Daniel took the letter. "A letter from Miss Whitaker?"

"Miss Whitaker, soon to be Mrs. Tanner," Esther said with a smile.

"Really?" Daniel scanned Agnes's spidery writing. "How wonderful!"

He grinned at Esther. "Paroxysms of delight? That sounds more like a disease than something good."

Esther laughed.

On April second, Richmond and Petersburg surrendered to Northern troops. Esther, at Peter's insistence, made her pudding cake for supper to celebrate, using some of the honey Mrs. Washburn had given her the year before.

After they were finished eating, Esther sat on the porch steps, patching holes in the knees of Peter's trousers. Daniel sat below her, snatching at Victoria's braids whenever she came within reach. She would dart in to touch him and then retreat out of range, giggling. He stood up once, and she ran off to the pasture where the twins were riding Triangle.

Esther grinned as Daniel sat back down. "You're not going to chase her?"

His eyes twinkled. "I was only stretching."

Esther's needle slowed. "Do you know what she told me this morning? She told me that she wanted to be like me when she grows up. I felt pleased at the time, but now that I've thought about it, I feel scared."

"Why scared?"

"Because I make a lot of mistakes." Esther stabbed her needle through the threadbare cloth. "What makes me a worthy example?"

"You help other people," Daniel said, shifting to face her. "You took care of David, hundreds of wounded soldiers, me—" He stopped. "Esther, did I ever tell you that Jack Mason was killed at Gettysburg?"

Esther's eyes widened. "No."

Daniel nodded. "When I joined my company at the battlefield, I found him slumped against a tree, calling out to the men to keep fighting. He'd been run through with a bayonet, but he was holding the company together for me like he promised while I took you back to your unit."

Daniel was silent for a moment, rubbing his hand over his forehead. "Right before Mason died, he said, 'Do you know what I want? I want another one of those cookies David's sister sent him.'"

Daniel went on, his voice quiet. "You've touched more people than you realized, Esther. I learned from the war that life is short, and people are more important than anything else. You seemed to realize that a long time ago, and the way you've taken care of others for as long as I've known you is very inspiring."

"Thank you." Esther blinked, feeling self-conscious. "Captain Armstrong, you wax quite eloquent."

Her tongue tripped over the q's in her words, and she covered her face with her hands. "I can't even talk right," she moaned.

Daniel laughed. "I didn't hear anything," he whispered. Then he continued in his normal voice, "I do wax quite eloquent. I should be a lawyer...or a preacher. Something to use my unique talents." He made a ridiculous face and bowed to an imaginary crowd.

Esther smiled, resuming her work.

Daniel stopped bowing and said thoughtfully, "So Richmond and Petersburg are evacuated. Didn't your father send you those letters from a prison in Petersburg?"

Esther stared at him for a moment. "Yes, but he said he might get transferred. Are you thinking he might be free now?" Her heart soared.

Daniel glanced at her strangely. "The prisons are overcrowded and disease-ridden, Esther." His voice was quiet. "After two years, your father might not still be alive."

Esther stood up, her legs trembling. "Why are you telling me this? To make me feel better?" Her voice rose. "Don't take my hope away, Daniel!"

Going inside, she slammed the door and plunked down on the living room sofa. She stared out the window, Peter's trousers forgotten on her lap. *Could he actually have died? Oh, Daddy!*

After several minutes she heard the door open and close, and Daniel came in and sat down beside her. She didn't look at him.

"I'm sorry, Esther." His voice was low. "I hope he's still alive too. Please don't be mad at me."

She turned to him, her face softening. "I'm not anymore. But I have to keep believing that he's alive, Daniel." She searched his eyes. "Until I know for sure that he isn't. He would do the same for me."

"So would I," Daniel murmured. "I understand, Esther."

30. Threadbare Trousers

Just over a week later on Monday morning, Esther was braiding Victoria's hair when she heard hoof beats pounding in the lane.

"Who could that be?" she wondered aloud, tying a ribbon at the end of the girl's second braid. "Come, let's go see."

Victoria took her hand and followed her outside.

Daniel was sliding off Triangle in the yard. He hollered, "Peter! Priscilla!"

The twins rushed out of the barn. "What? What happened?"

Daniel turned toward Esther, his grin nearly splitting his face. "The South surrendered!" he shouted. "On April ninth, yesterday morning. The war is over now!"

Esther's eyes widened. "Over?" she whispered, her chest feeling tight. "Really and truly over for good?"

"Really and truly over for good," Daniel repeated, laughing. "Careful now, your eyes are about to pop out."

"The war is over?" Priscilla's face lit up. "I must say, it was about time."

"Does that mean," Victoria began, but Peter interrupted her.

"I agree. It was about—"

Daniel clamped a hand on Peter's shoulder. "Let Victoria talk." He smiled down at Victoria. "Go ahead, Precious."

Victoria smiled back at him. "Does that mean all the soldiers can go home now?"

The ones who haven't been killed, Esther thought, sadness creeping over her.

"Yes," Daniel answered. "All the soldiers can go home now, because the war is over. The war is over!"

He caught her hands and pulled her around in a wild dance, following the twins' example. The two couples chased each other around and then joined hands and started skipping in a circle.

"Come on, Esther!" Daniel broke out of the ring, grabbed her hand, and pulled her in. "The war is over!"

Victoria and the twins said it with him, chanting it as they skipped.

Daniel flashed a grin at Esther. "Say it with us!" he commanded.

Esther laughed and obeyed. After a few more rounds, the circle broke up. Peter and Priscilla raced each other back to the barn, and Victoria slipped off into the house.

The last "The war is over!" chant died away as Esther walked over to Triangle and rubbed her nose.

"I'll put her away and help the twins finish the chores," Daniel offered, holding out his hand.

"Why were you in town so early in the morning?" Esther handed him the reins.

"Oh!" A sheepish look crossed Daniel's face. "Mr. Washburn came over and asked me to buy some medicine for Margaret's cough. But I forgot about it as soon as I rode into Kirksville and heard people saying that the South had surrendered. I'll have to go back."

Esther rubbed Triangle's forehead as he swung into the saddle. "I'll save some breakfast for you," she promised.

"Then I'll be sure to hurry." Daniel flashed her a smile, turning Triangle toward the road.

Five days later they heard that President Lincoln was dead, killed by an assassin's bullet. They were eating supper when Mr. Washburn brought the news, and as he drove away, they all stood on the porch, looking after him.

"What will happen now, Daniel?" Esther slid her arm around Victoria.

Daniel looked at the sky as if searching for an answer in the fluffy white clouds. "I suppose the vice president will be sworn in as the new president." He rubbed the back of his neck. "Life will go on."

"But what about the South?" Esther continued. "President Lincoln would have helped them rebuild their lives. They hurt themselves when they killed him."

"I'm sure not everyone in the South wanted Lincoln dead, Esther," Peter said from where he sat astride the railing. "Just like not everyone in the South upheld slavery."

Esther nodded and then frowned. "Peter, don't slide back and forth that way. You'll tear—"

There was a loud ripping sound. Peter looked chagrined, and Priscilla and Victoria snickered.

"Your trousers," Esther finished, a few seconds too late. She sighed. "Go inside and change so I can mend them."

"Yes, Esther." Peter carefully dismounted the railing and whisked through the door.

Esther sighed again. "Will he ever grow up?"

Daniel laughed. "Do you mean will he ever stop being hard on his clothes? It's doubtful. He's a boy, isn't he? Better resign yourself."

Esther made a face, and Priscilla snickered.

For the next two weeks Daniel and Peter worked from dawn to dusk, plowing and planting the fields. Daniel did the Sullivans' hay and cornfields with Triangle, and Peter did his father's with their team. Esther and Priscilla carried sandwiches and tea out to them every day at noon.

One evening they all sat on the porch steps after supper, watching the sun set behind the woods at the edge of the field.

"I love this farm," Daniel said, gazing at the barn and across the plowed fields. "It's the perfect size. Someday I'm going to own a farm like this, raise a family, and just…be a farmer."

He nodded his head as if settling it in his own mind. "That good feeling you get after a long day when you know your work should produce a good crop? There's nothing like it. How about it, Peter?"

Peter shook his head. "No," he said firmly. "I'm going to own a business. Like Mr. Taylor's General Store."

"A business, Peter?" Victoria pushed her head underneath his arm and wrinkled her nose at him. "How are you going to get a business?"

Peter traced her face with the end of her braid. "You work up from the bottom of the ladder," he told her. "First, you start by sweeping floors. Then you move to stocking shelves, then waiting on customers, and eventually, you get to handle the money and the books. The owner depends on you and cannot function without you. Then…"

Peter paused with a dramatic flourish of his hand and lowered his voice to a whisper. "The owner dies, leaving his store to you. And you have a business." He looked down and met Victoria's wide, blue gaze.

"Is Mr. Taylor going to die?" she demanded.

Peter tossed his head back, rolling his eyes. "No, dear sister, he's not. At least not anytime soon. That was merely an example. You could do it with any business, as long as you know that you have to start from the bottom."

"Brilliant, Peter!" Esther raised her eyebrows. "How *ever* did you come up with the concept of working your way up?"

"Oh, I got it from the army." Peter shrugged. "A private has to earn the position of a sergeant, then a lieutenant, a captain—" He motioned to Daniel. "Colonel, major, and finally, general. It's all about working your way up, as I said."

"But you were never with the army," Esther reminded him.

Daniel raised his hand where he was slouched against the porch railing. "He got all that from me. And a major comes before a colonel, not the other way around."

Peter's face reddened, and Priscilla burst out laughing.

Esther squeezed Peter's shoulder. "No matter where you got it from, Peter, I'm proud of you for realizing that all important positions have to be earned. It's not that much different than Daniel wanting to work hard as a farmer, and we need businessmen as well as farmers."

"Thanks, Esther," Peter mumbled. "At least someone believes in me."

He shot a significant glance at his twin. Priscilla was holding her sides and shaking with laughter.

Esther patted his shoulder. "Don't worry, Peter. She'll grow up sometime."

"Her? Grow up?" Peter repeated in disbelief. He moved his shoulder out of Esther's reach.

Esther grinned. "Yes, *her*. I have faith in her too."

"Peter," Daniel sat up and stretched. "Esther believes in everybody, whether they deserve it or not. That's part of what makes her so special."

Peter sniffed. "Yes, she believed you would get well when that doctor in Chambersburg didn't think you'd live."

Daniel leaned forward. "What do you mean? The doctor didn't think I would live?"

Peter wrapped Victoria's braid around her neck. "He said you weren't worth his time because you wouldn't pull through your fever. So Esther took out your bullet. I saw her testing her *knife*." He widened his eyes dramatically and poked Victoria.

"Stop it, Peter!" Victoria squirmed away. "Esther, I forgot to feed the chickens before supper."

"You took out my bullet, Esther?" Daniel stared at her, a strange look in his brown eyes.

"No one else would." Esther stood up, stepping past the twins to the ground. "And I couldn't let you die from the infection in your leg.

"Come, Victoria, I'll help you feed the chickens. Let's go before it gets any darker." Esther took Victoria's hand, hurrying away from the steps and the look on Daniel's face.

One night, Esther asked Victoria to kneel down in front of her chest of drawers. "I want to try combing your hair a different way," she said.

Victoria giggled with anticipation. "All right."

"Help me remember to pack your nightgown tomorrow morning before you leave," Esther told her. "We mustn't forget that."

The Washburns were going to be gone for six days visiting Mr. Washburn's parents, who lived in the northern part of the state. Esther had helped Victoria pack some clothes into the medium-sized trunk she was sharing with Priscilla, and Peter had stuffed his clothes into a crate, the same one he'd been living out of for the seven months at the Sullivan's house.

"There." Esther helped Victoria stand up so she could see herself in the looking glass. "What do you think?"

Victoria shrieked at the pile of hair on her head. "Esther, that looks horrible! Take it out right now."

Esther laughed and took out the pins. "Hold still. I'm going to try a French braid on you."

"What's a French braid?"

"This," Esther said when she was done. She handed Victoria a handheld looking glass so the girl could see the back of her head.

"That looks nice," Victoria breathed, turning her head from one side to the other. She lay down the looking glass and waltzed into the middle of the room. "Does a French braid make me look older, Esther?"

Esther tilted her head. "Why would you want to look older?"

Victoria shrugged and then burst out, "I'm tired of everyone treating me like a little girl. I'm almost ten! Well, you're not as bad as Mother and Priscilla."

"I'm sorry, Precious, but you're just so much fun to play with." Esther gave her a hug and then started tickling her.

"Esther!" Victoria shouted. She twisted out of Esther's reach and stomped across the floor. "You are mean," she pouted.

Esther laughed. "I'm sorry," she said. "That was sort of mean. Here, I'll take out your French braid, and I promise not to tickle you anymore."

When the French braid had been demolished, Victoria took the comb from Esther. "Let me comb your hair now."

"All right." Esther pulled the pins from her bun, letting her black hair tumble down. She climbed onto the bed and sat cross-legged with her back to Victoria. "I'll sit here so you can reach it."

Victoria gently pulled the comb through Esther's hair. "Your hair is pretty, Esther," she said.

Esther smiled. "Thank you."

Victoria dropped the comb and started tickling her.

"Victoria!" Esther lunged forward to break the younger girl's hold. "Stop it! You—" She turned, starting to laugh.

"I got you back."

Esther had never seen Victoria look so pleased. "You sure did."

She grabbed Victoria, and the younger girl tickled her again. Esther slapped her hands away, laughing.

Someone thumped at their door.

"Come in," Esther called, wiping her eyes. It could only be Priscilla.

Sure enough, Priscilla entered, a blanket wrapped around her shoulders and her light brown hair sticking up in a little poof.

Esther and Victoria took one look at her and dissolved into giggles again.

"Do you realize," Priscilla said in a disgruntled voice, her eyes blinking in the light from their lamp, "that I am trying to sleep? We have to leave tomorrow morning, and I need my rest. As do you, I might add. Do try to be quiet."

Esther choked back her laughter and nodded. "We'll go to bed now, Priscilla. Sorry for being so loud."

"Goodnight, then." Priscilla disappeared, closing the door loudly.

Esther rolled off the bed and raced to the door. "Priscilla?" she called, yanking it open. "Come back and let me comb your hair nicely before you go to bed. Please? It won't take long, I promise."

Priscilla, halfway into David's old room, frowned at Esther but shuffled back across the hall.

Esther pushed the door shut behind her. "What shall we do to her, Victoria?" she asked mischievously.

"Pile her hair up like you did mine." Victoria giggled. "That looked really horrible."

Priscilla, already kneeling down in front of the chest of drawers, harumphed. "Esther promised me something nice," she said confidently.

"That's right, I did." Esther began combing Priscilla's fine hair.

"All right, what do you think of that?" she asked, several minutes later. She'd made two braids along Priscilla's head and tied them with a ribbon where they met.

Priscilla examined herself. "That *is* nice," she said, turning to smile at Esther. "Thank you."

"It looks like a crown," Victoria observed. "Will you fix my hair like that now?"

"Maybe some other time." Esther finished combing out her own hair and quickly braided it. "Priscilla is right. We need to go to bed."

Priscilla climbed to her feet and hugged them both. "Goodnight."

Esther put on her nightgown while Victoria blew out the lamp, and then they both tumbled into bed. Victoria snuggled up to Esther, and Esther smoothed the younger girl's hair back from her face.

Victoria shifted. "Esther, why did God let your mama die?"

Esther froze. *What put that thought into her head?* "I don't know the answer to that question, Precious," she said after a moment. "I asked Dad about it once, and he said that since God is so much bigger than we are, we can't understand everything he lets happen."

She paused. "It's hard to trust that everything will be all right, and sometimes I feel upset at God. But that only makes me miserable. So I'm trying not to get upset, even though I don't understand why he let Mama die. All I know is that I miss her—so much."

Victoria snuggled closer, wrapping her arm around Esther's waist. "I'm sorry, Esther. I didn't mean to make you sad."

Esther smoothed Victoria's hair back from her face again. "I know you didn't," she whispered.

Silence filled the room for several minutes, and then Victoria whispered, "I was trying to imagine how I would feel if *my* mother died. I decided I didn't want that to happen. But I know you didn't want your mother to die either, so I was trying to figure out why God would take your mother to heaven and let mine keep on living. That's why I asked you…" She let her words trail off with a tiny sigh.

Esther swallowed hard. Victoria *was* growing up.

31. Together

The next morning, Esther watched the Washburns' team and wagon roll down the road. She sighed, missing her friends already. *What am I going to do by myself for six whole days?* she wondered.

Daniel had gone to stay at the Washburns and look after their animals while they were away.

Dad's room probably needs to be cleaned, Esther thought. *I should do it while Daniel is gone.*

She went inside to her parents' bedroom and pulled the quilts and linens off the bed to wash them. As she turned to go out, she caught sight of something wedged between the chest of drawers and the wall. Reaching down, she wiggled out a piece of paper. Unfolding it, she scanned the few lines.

Dear Sir:

In response to the letter you sent me on April fifth, inquir-
ing after the whereabouts of a Richard Sullivan, I regret
to inform you that the records of the prisoners here are
incomplete. I have no knowledge of any Richard Sullivan,
living or dead.

Esther stared at the letter, leaning against the chest of drawers. *So we still don't know anything more. No wonder Daniel didn't
tell me. But he tried to find out.*

Tears stung her eyes as she folded the letter. Forgetting about
the pile of laundry, she went upstairs to add the letter to the collection in her top drawer. The interlocking hearts on her mother's
necklace gleamed, and Esther frowned.

*I haven't visited Mama's grave since last autumn when I came
home. And this is already the sixth of May.*

Esther went to the barn for a hand sickle and then headed for
the tiny meadow beside the woods where her mother and David
had been buried. Finding the wooden crosses that marked the
graves, she trimmed away the weeds.

Mama always found a way to make dull things enjoyable, she
thought, *whether it was shelling peas, doing the wash, or spreading
mulch on the garden.* Remembering her mother's praise the first
time she cooked a meal by herself, made her first dress, and knitted her first stocking, Esther started crying.

"Mama," she whimpered, wrapping her arms around herself.
"Mama, I miss you."

She sniffed and wiped her eyes, touching the wooden cross. "I
love you, Mama," she whispered. "And I've been trying to go on
with my life, like you wanted me to."

*I'm not sure how to do that, though, since Dad and David are gone
now too,* she thought. *I'm all alone.*

But that wasn't true. She had the Washburns and—

Hearing footsteps, she turned. There stood Daniel, hands behind his back, his lopsided grin fading as he saw her tear-stained face.

And him, she thought, smiling a little. "Hello, Daniel."

He cleared his throat. "I wanted to talk to you about something, but—" He paused. "Esther, if you want to be left alone, tell me, and I'll go away."

She cut down the last clump of weeds. "No, it's all right. You can stay."

"Are you sure? You're not being polite?" His expression was concerned, but his eyes were twinkling.

She grinned. "Am I ever polite?"

"Oh, yes." He dropped to his knees, his voice earnest. "You are the most wonderful person I—" He paused and started over. "You are a wonderful person, and I want to thank you again for everything you've done for me. Now that Whirlwind, Spitfire, and Precious are gone, I feel I can breathe again."

Esther laughed. Those were his nicknames for Peter, Priscilla, and Victoria.

"You didn't let me thank you properly when Peter told all of us how you saved my life in Chambersburg," Daniel continued, "so I decided to wait on the flowers."

"The flowers?" Esther repeated.

Daniel pulled a bouquet of wild phlox from behind his back and held it out to her. "I couldn't find any before today," he explained.

"Oh, Daniel, these are my favorite! I love the way they smell."

Esther took the bouquet and buried her nose in the purple, sweet-smelling flowers as he added, "Thank you, Little Birdie."

Esther glanced up and saw him biting his lip as he watched her. She lowered the bouquet and smiled at the flowers. "You're welcome," she said. "It was an honor to care for you. Even if you did growl at me sometimes."

Daniel laughed. "Will you go to church with me tomorrow?"

"Of course." She smelled the flowers again and divided them into two bunches. "You don't mind, do you?" she asked Daniel, laying one on each of the graves.

"No."

Esther straightened. "Without the Washburns here, I miss my own family more."

"I've been praying for your dad to come home," Daniel said. "Maybe he has a long way to travel and just hasn't made it back yet."

"Do you think?" she whispered. "I've been praying more for him lately too."

Daniel shrugged, and she rubbed her right arm above her elbow.

"Is that where the bullet hit you?" he asked. "Does it hurt a lot?"

She shook her head. "My arm is only hurting because I moved the big crocks in the springhouse to make room for this morning's milk. My back is sore too."

"No more moving crocks, then," Daniel ordered. "Or I'll have to take disciplinary measures."

"Daniel...Armstrong!" Esther sputtered. "What's your middle name? I want to scold you with your full name."

He looked down, picking at a piece of grass. "I don't like my middle name."

"What is it?"

He sighed. "Caleb."

"Caleb?" she repeated. "What's wrong with Caleb? Daniel Caleb Armstrong. I like it."

He shrugged, ripping the grass to shreds. "I just always liked my brother's middle name better."

"Ethan? What's his middle name?"

"Randall."

Esther repeated that to herself. "Ethan Randall Armstrong. That's nice. But it wouldn't fit with your name. Daniel Randall Armstrong. Too many *l*s. I like Caleb much better."

Daniel waved both hands in front of his face. "All right, all right. Enough about my middle name. What's yours?"

"Elizabeth."

A smile spread across Daniel's face. "Esther Elizabeth Sullivan. That is the prettiest name I have ever heard. Other than my mother's."

She smiled. "What was your mother's name?"

"Marianna Rachelle."

"That *is* pretty," Esther said softly. "Daniel, I hardly know anything about your family, other than Ethan and Molly. Tell me about your parents."

"My father had a weak heart. He died when I was four." Daniel picked another piece of grass, twirling it between two fingers. "I don't really remember him. Ethan was more like a father to me, even though he is only nine years older."

Daniel paused. "My mother was always praying for me," he continued. "And for Ethan too. She was so committed to seeing us succeed.

"One time when I was around ten, my friends and I made fun of an African boy." He shook his head with a sheepish smile. "She took me for a walk, and when we came to a meadow, she sat me down and told me about the Daniel in the Bible that she had named me after. How he stood up for what was right, even though he got thrown in the lions' den for doing it.

"She said, 'Daniel, God made that African boy just the same as he made you, and he wants you to treat each other nicely. Only the color of your skin is different. I want you to remember the Daniel from the Bible and be just like him. Stand up for what you know is right, even if you're the only one doing it. And treat everyone the way you want to be treated, even if they look or act differently than you.'"

Daniel was silent for a moment. "I've always remembered that," he said, his voice husky. "It was part of the reason I organized my own company and joined the army. I believed that the slaves should be as free as everyone else."

"And now they are," Esther said. "Did you grow up in Ohio?" she asked after a bit.

"No, we lived here in Pennsylvania." Daniel rubbed his face. "But Mother died after Ethan and Molly moved to Ohio, and I sold our house when I enlisted."

"I wish I could have met your mother," Esther said, feeling the sun on her back and squinting upward. "It's noon," she announced. "Will you stay to lunch?"

"I probably shouldn't. You haven't had time to make anything."

"Oh, I was planning to have leftovers from last night's supper," Esther reassured him. "But I know I can't eat all of it by myself. Please say you'll stay and help me." She tilted her head and gave him a pleading smile.

He frowned. "Don't give me that look. You don't have to try that hard to convince me. I'll stay."

Then he grinned and jumped to his feet. "Race you to the house," he called, dashing off.

"Daniel!" Clambering to her feet, she picked up the hand sickle and ran after him, even though she knew she wouldn't win.

As she passed the cornfield, she noticed that he wasn't as far ahead anymore, and soon she could tell that he was letting her catch up.

"I don't want you to let me beat you!" she hollered, slowing down.

"Keep running," he called over his shoulder, nearly jogging in place. "I'm not letting you beat me."

She caught up with him, and he reached for her hand. "Let's finish together," he panted, his brown hair flopping over his forehead.

Esther nodded, grinning, and took his hand. They were close to the porch steps by now, and just before they reached them, Daniel pulled back on her hand. She stopped and glanced at him, her breath coming in short gasps.

With a triumphant smile, he stretched their arms out so their fingers touched the first step at the same time. "Together," he said.

Esther gazed at him for a moment, her smile fading. The look in his eyes made her heart beat faster, even though it was already pounding from her run. Slowly, she pulled her hand out of his.

"I'm going to get the food from the springhouse, and you can set the table," she said finally, wrenching her gaze away.

"Set the table?" he repeated. "That's Victoria's—"

"She isn't here." Esther stepped past him. She could feel him watching her until she ducked into the springhouse.

Dipping her fingers into the water running through the stone trough, Esther put them to her face, letting the moisture cool her hot cheeks. A scene from a week ago flashed through her mind.

She and Priscilla had been making bread in the kitchen when Daniel and Peter burst into the house, shouting, "The planting is done! Let's celebrate!"

Peter had squeezed his twin in an ecstatic hug, and Daniel had grabbed Esther's floury hands with his dirty ones, spinning her around.

"Daniel." She had laughed. "You're getting me dirty, and I'm not done kneading the bread."

"I'm sorry. But I'm so happy I could do it again."

In the springhouse Esther sank down on the side of the stone trough, remembering the look in Daniel's eyes. It had been the same as when he said, "Together."

"This is so confusing," she whispered. "I wish Dad would be here. Dear God, please, please send him home, and help me know what to do."

Her mother's words from long ago rang in her mind. *God might not answer your prayers the way you want him to.*

Esther sighed. "I know I shouldn't be upset at you for not answering my prayers, God," she whispered, "but I want him to come home so badly."

Standing up, she took the leftover chicken and fresh peas from the cooling trough and went back to the house.

Daniel opened the door for her. "I was beginning to think you had fallen into the creek."

"I was just catching my breath," she told him, placing the food on the neatly set table. "Let's eat. Before it gets cold."

He laughed at the irony of her words.

After they had finished eating, Daniel helped her wash the few dishes they'd used. "I should go check the cut on Daisy's leg," he said, flinging his towel over the wash tub. "I put some salve on it this morning and wrapped it up, but she likes to rub off the bandage."

"I hope it heals soon," Esther said, wiping her hands on her apron.

Daniel nodded. "So do I. I'll see you tomorrow."

The next morning as Esther was dressing for church, she opened the top drawer and took out her mother's necklace. *This will look lovely with my dress,* she thought.

The dress was her mother's also, one of the ones she and her father had packed into a trunk. She had gotten it out and altered it the week before. It was the same blue dress her mother had worn the day they had their photograph taken, and Esther had found a straw bonnet to wear with it.

She fastened the necklace at the back of her neck under her pinned-up hair and stared at her reflection in the looking glass. The interlocking silver hearts sparkled in the morning sunlight, and she caught her breath, remembering the many times her mother had worn it.

"Mama, I wish I could see you again," she whispered.

Hearing hoof beats, she pushed back her blue and white curtain to look out the window. Daniel was out by the barn, hitching Triangle to the wagon.

"Where did we put them?" she muttered, rummaging through one of her mother's trunks. "Oh, here they are." She held up her mother's pair of white gloves and pulled them on, surprised at how well they fit. She hurried downstairs, her skirts swishing.

"Good morning, Daniel," she called, walking toward the barn. "Isn't the sky beautiful?"

"Yes, it is." Daniel turned from adjusting Triangle's bridle, a startled expression crossing his face.

"What?" Esther demanded. "Is something wrong with my bonnet? What are you staring at?"

He looked like he was holding back a smile, but all he said was, "Your locket's crooked."

"It's not a locket. It's a necklace." Esther reached up to finger it. "It was Mama's. Dad gave it to me after she died. He said she was planning to give it to me on my sixteenth birthday."

Daniel walked the reins back to the wagon. "If they could, I'm sure your parents would tell you how proud they are of you, Esther." His voice was quiet as he held out his hand to help her up to the wagon seat. "And how much of a lady you've become. You look stunning this morning in that dress."

She smiled even as tears pricked the corners of her eyes and took his hand. "Thank you."

32. David's Letter

They were almost home after the church service when Triangle slowed, her ears twitching.

Esther had been about to ask Daniel if he would stay to Sunday dinner, but instead she said, "What is the matter?"

"I don't know." Daniel wrinkled his forehead. "She usually tries to go faster right about here."

Triangle threw up her head and whinnied, breaking into a rough, unsteady canter as the house came into view.

Esther clutched the seat. "She doesn't usually go this fast, though!" she exclaimed, irritated. "Triangle, slow down!"

Triangle flicked one ear backward, and her gait became smoother, but she continued to charge up the road at a canter. Daniel braced his feet against the wagon's floorboards and gripped the reins, muttering something about temperamental females.

As they turned in the lane, Esther pushed a wind-blown curl out of her face and glanced at the house. A man was walking to the porch steps, and at the sound of Triangle's hoof beats, he turned to look at them.

Esther blinked. Then she gasped, her heart racing. "It's Dad!" she whispered, clutching Daniel's arm.

Tears sprang to her eyes as Triangle clattered up beside the porch steps and stopped. Esther jumped to the ground, nearly catching her skirts in the wheel, and rushed toward her father.

"Dad!"

He had been staring at them, but at the sound of her voice, he stepped forward, opening his arms wide. "Esther? Is it really you?"

"Yes, Dad." Esther hugged him, wincing at how thin he was. "It's really me."

"I missed you more than I can say," he murmured, pulling back to look at her. "Sweetheart, you've changed so much in two years. You're all grown up."

Esther shook her head and flung her arms round his neck again, a lump forming in her throat. "No, Daddy," she whispered. "I'm still your little girl."

She felt him take a quick breath. "And you always will be," he said, his arms tightening around her.

They held each other for a long time, and Esther felt the fragments of her life settle into place. *Mama and David are gone forever, but oh, God, thank you for sending Dad back to me!*

At last she released him and stepped back, pulling her handkerchief out of her sleeve. Her father rubbed his shirtsleeve across his eyes.

"Daniel Armstrong?" he exclaimed as Daniel climbed down from the wagon. "I certainly didn't expect to find you here."

Esther took her father's arm. "It's a long story, Dad. Let's go inside and sit down before I tell you. Daniel will come in and tell his part of it too. Won't you?" She glanced at Daniel.

Daniel nodded. "I'll unhitch Triangle and be right in."

"Triangle?" Her father stepped closer to the horse. "When did you get her back?"

Esther pulled on his arm, grinning. "Come inside, Dad. We'll tell you everything."

She helped him inside, and he gazed around the dining room. "Esther, why is he here? Did you marry him?"

Esther stared at her father, suddenly feeling hot all over. "Dad! He is staying at the Washburns to take care of their animals while they are visiting Mr. Washburn's parents."

Removing her gloves, she thought she saw her father trying to hide a smile. She took a deep breath. "I went to church with him this morning, and he was bringing me home."

She went into the kitchen, tied an apron over her dress, and began making dinner, pulling out a chair for her father.

Before long Daniel came in and sat down, and her father tapped his fingers on the table.

"All right, Esther," he said. "Can you talk while you work? Tell me what happened since I left. Tell me *everything*."

Esther flashed him a smile, answering the twinkle in his eyes, and told him all she could remember. Daniel added a lot also, and by the time they were both finished, all of them were done eating and had been sitting at the table for two hours.

Esther's father reached over and squeezed her hand. "I'm so glad God kept you safe through all of that."

Esther grinned. "Yes, after my exciting time with the army, these last few months have been quite peaceful."

"They have also been life-changing. For me, at least." Daniel turned to her father. "I gave my life to God three months ago."

"You did?" Her father beamed. "That is wonderful!"

He ran a hand through his hair, now mostly gray, and Esther touched his arm. "Tell us what happened to you, Dad."

"There's not that much to tell," her father said slowly. "I think I wrote you that I took care of the cavalry's horses while I was with the army. After the Confederates captured me, they marched me down to Petersburg with hundreds of other prisoners.

"I was in prison there until this spring when the Union army took the town, and we were freed. I stayed with a kind family in Maryland for three weeks until I had enough strength to travel the rest of the way here." He smiled at Esther. "God answered my prayers and brought me home to you."

Daniel stood up. "I'm going to head back to the Washburns now. Thank you for dinner, Esther."

"You're welcome. Thank you for taking me to church." She stood up to open the door for him. "Good-bye."

"Daniel?" Esther's father leaned back in his chair. "Thank you for taking such good care of my daughter."

"Actually, sir," Daniel glanced at Esther, "it was her taking care of me."

"You both took care of each other," Esther's father said. "So thank you."

Daniel nodded and went out. "Good-bye, Esther."

She closed the door and turned to her father. "Dad, I'll put fresh linens on your bed right away, and you can rest until suppertime."

He stood up slowly and stretched. "In my own bed? Oh, Esther, that sounds wonderful."

As Esther finished making the bed in her parents' room, she heard the door open and close. Going to the dining room, she glanced out the window and saw her father. "Dad?" she whispered.

She watched him go down the porch steps as slowly as an old man. When he reached the bottom, he straightened and started off across the field, his steps unsteady.

Esther drew in a quick breath. Opening the door, she went out onto the porch and watched him, praying he wouldn't try to climb the rock.

He walked past the rock, and tears gathered in Esther's eyes as he fell on his knees beside her mother's grave. When he pushed himself to his feet and stumbled back toward the house, she ran to meet him and helped him to bed, her heart breaking at the way he held on to her to keep from falling.

Although she had missed them as soon as they left, Esther was glad, for her father's sake, the Washburns were away. Several days of rest and good food made him much stronger. When they came home on Friday, he enjoyed seeing them, even with all their noise and attention.

Peter, Priscilla, and Victoria moved their things back to their own house, and Esther missed them more than she thought was reasonable, since they were still her neighbors. The Washburns had insisted that Daniel stay with them, and she missed him the most.

Three days later, as Esther was wiping the dinner crumbs from the table, her father came out of his bedroom. She looked up as he tapped the envelope he held.

"Esther, do you remember David asking me to give you a letter before he died?"

Esther stopped swishing the dishrag across the table. "Yes, I do," she said slowly.

Her father handed her the envelope. "He was going to give it to you on your next birthday or at the end of the war, whichever came first." He smiled. "I missed both those dates, and I'm sorry. I'll finish wiping the table so you can go read it now."

Esther turned the envelope over and saw the words, "Little Birdie." Tears sprang to her eyes at the sight of her brother's handwriting.

"Thanks, Dad," she whispered before the lump in her throat made it impossible to speak. Turning, she went outside to David's grave.

The bouquet of wild phlox from Daniel that she'd put beside the cross was withered, and she flung it away before sitting down. Sliding a finger under the envelope flap, she took out the letter and unfolded it.

December 1862

Dear Esther,

Do you remember our talk about how God makes his final decision on people? It was only yesterday, so it is very clear in my mind as I am writing, but I am not sure when you will read this. I want God's final decision on you to be good, so I beg you, if you haven't already, put your faith in Jesus and ask him to make you holy so you can spend eternity with him. That is the only way to heaven.

Little Birdie, you are such a special girl, and I love you so much. When the time comes for each of us to get married and live our own lives, I will miss being with you. (Do you think we will ever get married?)

Always remember that the most important thing in life is to love God and serve other people. I'm going to go serve Dad by beating him at checkers to keep him humble, so I will sign off now.

I remain forever your devoted servant and loving brother,

David

Esther swallowed hard against the ache in her heart, envisioning her brother's twinkling blue eyes and teasing grin. A tear trickled down her cheek as she sat there, staring at the letter. She thought of her prayers over the last three years and was suddenly ashamed, realizing how selfish she had been.

I wanted God to keep me safe, bring Dad home, and heal Daniel, she reflected. *But I hardly ever thanked him for taking care of me. I ignored him unless I wanted something.*

"Dear God, I am sorry for being so selfish," she whispered, looking up over the trees. "If I had only looked past my hurt, the way Dad told me to, I would have seen how much you truly love me. Please forgive me for being upset with you and ignoring you all these years. Thank you for sending your Son to die for my sins. Jesus, please come into my heart and make me holy."

She squeezed her eyes shut and bowed her head, feeling peace and happiness steal over her. Opening her eyes, she beamed up into the blue, blue sky. "Thank you, God!"

Now she knew what David had meant when he said he felt clean. She wanted to tell somebody.

Folding the letter, she sprang to her feet and dashed toward the house. "Dad?" she called, bursting through the door. The house was silent.

She dropped the letter on the table and ran out to the barn. "Dad!"

"I'm over here, Esther."

She paused inside the door until her eyes adjusted to the dimness and then started forward again when she caught sight of him cleaning Triangle's stall. "Daddy, I gave my heart to God!"

"You did?" He straightened, leaning the pitchfork against the wall. "Oh, Esther, I'm so glad!" He stepped out of the stall and hugged her, kissing the top of her head.

They stood there for a moment, and he said, "Was it because of David's letter?"

Esther nodded against his chest. "I don't know why I was so stubborn, Dad." She pulled back to look up at him. "I saw the peace and joy David and Daniel had after giving their lives to God. I even felt envious. But it wasn't until I read David's letter that I realized how selfish and rude I've been to God. I expected him to answer my prayers, even though I was upset at him when Mama and David died and you were taken. I ignored him the rest of the time. I feel so unworthy of his forgiveness."

Her father shook his head, smiling. "None of us deserve God's forgiveness, Esther, or his love. I am so grateful he does not treat us according to our worthiness."

Esther nodded again. "I wish I had let go of my resentment sooner," she said after a minute. "I would have been so much happier."

She took his hand. "Thank you for praying for me all this time, Dad. After David died and you were taken, I felt like I was drowning and your prayers were my lifeline."

"It was the best thing I could do for you, sweetheart." He squeezed her hand. "Prayer is the most powerful weapon God's children have—more powerful than a cannon. Never forget that."

As Esther was scrubbing the kitchen floor that afternoon, she heard someone knocking. Climbing to her feet, she wiped her hands on her apron and went to answer the door.

She smiled when she saw who it was. "Hello, Daniel. Come in."

He stepped inside. "Hello, Esther. You're wearing your hair differently, aren't you? I like it."

Esther's forehead wrinkled, and she reached up to touch the braids wound around her head. "Oh, yes. It's how Dad remembers me, and it helps him not have so many things to adjust to."

Daniel nodded.

"And, Daniel..." She clasped her hands under her chin, beaming with excitement. "I gave my heart to Jesus."

His eyes lit up. "You did? Really?"

She nodded. "This afternoon."

For a moment she thought his elated grin might split his face. He whirled and strode to the living room, taking the Bible from the mantel. She followed and sat down on the sofa beside him.

"I want to show you a verse in Hebrews." He found the place and read it aloud. "'For it became him, for whom are all things, and by whom are all things, in bringing many sons unto glory, to make the captain of their salvation perfect through sufferings.'

"Jesus is the captain of our salvation, Esther. Now we are under the same captain." He smiled at her. "I'm so happy for you. I've been praying for this ever since I gave my life to God."

"You have?" Esther asked. Maybe her father's prayers hadn't been the only strands in her lifeline.

"Yes, and for Whirlwind and Spitfire too."

Esther grinned. "I'll help you pray for them. Dad says prayer is even more powerful than a cannon, but I don't like that comparison. I've seen too much of what guns do."

Daniel glanced up at her and then back to the Bible in his lap, fingering the pages. "So have I."

She was silent a moment, touching the scar above her right elbow. "Daniel, how do you deal with your memories?"

He glanced up at her again with a questioning look in his brown eyes, and she went on. "Sometimes when I close my eyes, I see the piles of arms and legs that the doctors amputated. Even though it's been almost a year, it still makes me sick to my stomach. David told me once that he forced himself to ignore the suffering and dying to keep from losing his mind.

"I had a nightmare about that Confederate sniper shooting at you not long after we got home." She paused, twisting her apron string. "I dreamed that I didn't get to you in time and the bullet went straight through your heart. You cried out, and I screamed, waking myself up. It was so realistic that I ran downstairs to make sure you were still alive."

Esther took a deep breath, remembering how relieved she'd been to find Daniel asleep. She lifted her head to meet his eyes. "I don't think I'll ever forget what I saw in those hospitals. And I'm sure you saw worse things on the battlefield. Does it ever bother you?"

Daniel sat back and raked his fingers through his hair. "Yes," he said slowly. "The first several battles I was in were the worst. Hearing the cries of men who were shot, seeing the wounded and the flies on dead horses and soldiers—" He paused. "Every time I saw a dead soldier, I almost felt guilty for being alive. I wondered, why them and not me?

"I tried to endure the horror of it all, hoping it would end soon. But it didn't! It kept going, and neither side was winning. I think most of us had forgotten what we were fighting about, whether it was freeing the slaves or upholding states' rights. When we lined up facing each other, it felt like we were only trying to see which side could kill the most men first. I felt dirty every time I pulled the trigger."

"You did?" Esther whispered. "I didn't know that. I hated what you were doing, but I couldn't tell you then. Remember when I apologized for knocking away your pistol after I was shot?"

Daniel nodded. "I wondered if you meant that," he said quietly.

Esther looked down at her hands. "I didn't. I had already watched Mama and David die, and I wanted to never see another person die, not even a Rebel." She shrugged. "But I did. And it hurt me every time."

Daniel swallowed hard. "I was hurt differently. The first few times I shot a Rebel soldier, I did what you said David did and forced myself not to think about it. But I hurt myself when I became calloused to all the killing. I didn't feel as guilty, but I couldn't feel anyone else's pain as much either.

"Then you came." The corner of his mouth turned up in a half smile. "I knew what you had been through, and yet you could still feel. You wanted to save others, even the Rebel who shot you. I was so ashamed of myself that day."

Daniel reached over to squeeze Esther's hand. "Your motives were so much better than mine, so pure. Each battle and skirmish after that was terrible for me. I couldn't shake the sense of wrongness in it all. That's when I applied for my discharge. After I gave my life to God, he took away my guilt and gave me peace."

David said the same thing, Esther thought, watching the tense lines fade from Daniel's forehead.

"I still feel guilty sometimes," Daniel went on, "and I will always have my memories. But when they torment me, I give them to God. He promised to take my sins as far away as the east is from the west. He takes my guilt and gives me peace in return."

Esther sat quietly for a moment. "Thank you, Daniel," she said at last. "Ever since I came home, I've been trying to forget what I've seen. But it hasn't worked."

Daniel rubbed his scar. "I've come to realize that God wants us to learn from our past, not forget it. He can use everything in our lives to help us become better people. I'm still amazed that he loves me after what I've done, and it makes me want to serve him every day!"

Esther's heart beat faster, stirred by the enthusiasm on his face. She nodded, starting to smile. "His forgiveness makes me feel like I'm really alive for the first time."

Her father came in from the barn then and asked Daniel to stay for supper.

"All right," Daniel said. "I should probably run over and let Mrs. Washburn know, though." He headed for the door.

Esther followed him. "Daniel, I blurted out my good news as soon as you arrived and never even asked why you'd come. I'm sorry."

He turned to face her as he opened the door. "Don't apologize. I was thrilled to hear your news. And to be honest, the only reason I came over was to see you." He smiled at her and went out.

Esther stared out the window after him as her father came up. He gave her a little grin, raising his eyebrows, but didn't say anything.

33. Her Other Heart

"Daddy, what is love?"

Esther and her father were sitting on the porch steps the next night, and at her question, he turned to look at her. After a moment he said, "Bring me the Bible."

Esther fetched it from the mantel and sat back down beside him.

"Read First Corinthians thirteen, verses one through seven," he told her. "And the first three words in verse eight."

Esther flipped pages until she found the place. She sped through the part that defined love as the most important thing to have and slowed down where it said love is patient, kind, humble, unselfish, and never-failing.

When she finished she closed the book and took a deep breath. "I guess that one little word means even more than I thought."

Her father smiled at her. "That is love according to the Bible. It is a sacrificial commitment to do what is best for others."

He gazed out across the field toward the graves near the rock. "Esther," he said slowly, "why you are asking me about love?"

Esther looked down, her thoughts tumbling over each other. "Because I—"

She stopped and raised her eyes to his, evaluating her feelings by the Bible's definition of love. "Daniel has been my best friend for these last eight months, and I—" She touched her necklace. "I think he's my other heart.

"But even though I love him, it's not up to me. I don't know what to think while I'm waiting." She stopped and rubbed her face, her hands trembling. "What should I do? I don't know how to deal with these emotions."

"Oh, Esther." Her father took her hands, pulling them away from her face. "I wish I hadn't missed it."

She drew back. "Missed what?"

"The time when you changed from a girl to a woman." His eyes softened. "You're still my little girl, but you are also a woman now. I love you so much, and I'm proud of the way you kept going, despite everything you went through. Mama would be too."

He smiled at her, squeezing her hands gently. "If Daniel is your other heart, God will bring you together. Psalm thirty-seven says, 'Commit your way unto the Lord, trust also in him, and he will give you the desires of your heart.' Isn't that a wonderful promise?"

"Yes, it is. Thank you, Daddy."

She scooted closer to lay her head on his shoulder, and he put his arm around her.

After Esther finished the dinner dishes two days later, she walked past the fields to the woods. Reaching the bridge that spanned the creek, she sat down on its edge. She looked beyond the green, leafy trees to the blue sky, swinging her feet above the water.

"Thank you, God, for this beautiful day," she whispered, listening to the rippling of the creek. A wren trilled, teetering on a branch in front of her. When it flew off, she turned to see Daniel walking up the trail.

He smiled. "May I join you?"

She nodded and returned his smile, watching the sunlight play over his face.

He dropped to the bridge beside her, sitting cross-legged. "I managed to escape Peter." He held out a white envelope. "Here you are. I'm delivering your latest letter, since I know you're quite fond of receiving them. If you like it, you can add it to that extensive collection you have in your top drawer.

"And I didn't snoop, either," he added, when she started frowning at him. "You told me about it once."

"I did?" Esther's frown disappeared, and she took the letter from him. Her name was scrawled on the back.

She glanced at Daniel and, opening the envelope, took out the slip of paper inside. Unfolding it, she read five words.

Esther, will you marry me?

For a moment she forgot to breathe. The letter slipped from her fingers, and Daniel reached out to catch it, half-crushing it before it was safely in his hand.

Esther drew back a little, staring at him. "You...really want me?" she stammered. She'd wished for this very thing, but now that it was happening, she didn't know what to say.

"Yes, Esther, I do." His eyes had that "together" look again.

"But...you need to... I mean, Dad—"

She took a deep breath, and Daniel said, "I asked your father for your hand in marriage last night, Esther."

"What did he say?" she whispered, remembering their talk on the porch steps.

Daniel tipped his head, his forehead wrinkling. "He said, 'Of course you may have her hand, Daniel. You already have her heart.'"

Esther looked down, wishing she didn't blush so easily. "Tattletale," she muttered.

Daniel glanced up quickly, searching her face. "It's true, then?"

She put her hands to her flaming cheeks for a moment and then dropped them. "Yes," she said simply, beaming at him.

He smiled back at her for a long moment. "Now that you know I've asked for your hand," he said softly, "will you take mine?"

Esther tore her gaze away from his eyes and stared at the hand he held out to her. "Yes," she whispered again, placing her trembling hand in his.

He closed his fingers over hers. "Did you really say yes?"

She wiped happy tears from her eyes. "Yes, Daniel. I'll marry you.

"Don't fall into the creek," she added when he whooped and threw up his arms.

"I won't." He handed her the letter and shifted, thrusting his legs over the edge to dangle beside hers. "I've wanted to ask you for a long time now, but I was waiting until we were both serving God under the same captain." He grimaced. "The waiting was hard."

"But it's over now." Esther smoothed her skirt, her thoughts racing ahead. "We can set a date for our wedding!" She turned to him, almost shyly. "Can we get married on my mother's birthday?"

He grinned at her and sprang to his feet, holding out his hand. "I don't care when we get married, as long as it's soon. Let's go tell your father."

🌿

Nearly three weeks later, Esther felt like cheering as she and Daniel rode away from the church in town on Triangle.

I'm married now! She fingered the lacy sleeve of what had been her mother's wedding dress. Lydia and Priscilla had helped her alter it one afternoon.

"Good-bye, Dad," she called, waving at him. He was planning to stay the night with the Washburns so they could have the whole house to themselves.

Her father waved back from where he stood on the church steps with the Washburns and their other friends and neighbors. "Good-bye. I'll see you both tomorrow."

"Esther, are you sure you don't want to ride astride?" Daniel asked. "The blanket will keep your dress clean, and then you wouldn't have to worry about sliding off."

Esther shook her head. "Not in this dress." She smiled at him. "And I'm not worried, because I know you wouldn't let me fall."

He laughed, pulling her a little closer. "You're right."

Then he shook his head, his expression softening. "Esther, I can hardly believe that God gave me such a sensitive, loving wife. I promise that with his help I will work hard to be the man you deserve."

Esther gazed up at him. "You already are a good man, Daniel." A thrill ran through her at the joy of spending the rest of her life with him.

She held up her necklace. "One of these hearts stands for me, Daniel, and the other one is for you." She flashed him a delighted smile. "You are my other heart."

He tipped his head, raising his eyebrows. "I guess I was wrong."

Wrong? Esther pulled back. "About what?"

"Remember at Rock Creek when you asked me not to die? I always thought you looked so beautiful then, but—"

"Daniel! At Rock Creek?" She stared at him. "I had just cried for who knows how long. I didn't look beautiful."

"You did to me. It was so hard to leave you there alone when I wanted to protect you." He smiled and touched the braids crowning her head. "But you're even more beautiful today."

"Thank you." She returned his smile and noticed the houses they were passing.

"I'm glad we are staying here in Kirksville. Now that Dad is home, I couldn't bear to move away."

Daniel nodded and shrugged. "I don't have a house of my own to offer you, and yes, your father is still recovering and needs to have you around.

"But he agrees with me that we should have some time to ourselves right now, and that means we have to go somewhere away from our wonderful neighbors."

He grinned at her. "Maybe I should take you to Ohio so you can meet Ethan and Molly and their family. What would you say to that? We'll ask Peter and Priscilla to stay with your father while we're gone. By the time he starts to miss us, we'll be back. How does that sound?"

"It sounds fantastic!" Esther beamed. "Daniel, I love how you always manage to please everybody."

He grinned. "As long as you're pleased, I'm satisfied. And that reminds me. There is something I've been wanting to tell you."

She smiled at him, her heart overflowing with happiness. "What is that?"

Daniel cupped her chin with his free hand and kissed her. "I love you, Little Birdie."

CPSIA information can be obtained
at www.ICGtesting.com
Printed in the USA
BVOW06s0105060917

493943BV00016B/131/P